The Other Italians

written by
David Mercaldo PhD

In conjunction with
Paperclip Press®

Bibliographic Information

The Other Italians

Published by:
Paperclip Press, 1603 Belvue Drive, Forest Hill, MD 21050
410-838-8264 / paperclippress.com

For distribution information please contact sales@paperclippress.com

Related Sites:
http://www.davidmercaldo.com
http://www.paperclippress.com
http://www.theotheritalians.com
1. History, 2. Theology 3. Italians, 4. Immigration

First Edition, August 2014 / PSGP / R2

Library of Congress Control Number: 2014948908

ISBN 978-0-9666187-5-4

$15.99
ISBN 978-0-9666187-5-4
51599>

9 780966 618754

For book events and speaking engagements contact
David Mercaldo, PhD at david@davidmercaldo.com

Contents

About the Author

David Mercaldo, who holds a PhD in childhood neurological behavior, is a prolific writer on such topics as education, politics, finance and drama, and travels nationwide as a motivational speaker to schools, colleges, civic organizations and business groups. This educator, playwright and author has given us such acclaimed works as **Ferry** (as in Staten Island), **Seamstress**, **Famiglia** and a children's book, **Little Boy Boo** (the adventures of a Yorkshire terrier who thought he was a boy), and is co-author of **Officer's Oath**. Theater goers have been entertained by his plays: Fathra, Apartment to Let, Eyewitness and a host of others.

Reflections

"This is a book about an organization that has had a profound influence on the history and culture of those individuals of Italian heritage and ancestry. David Mercaldo has dedicated himself to years of research, and in the words of critic and playwright ("NINE"), Mario Fratti, "he has now a new, daring book," and further confesses that, for many years Italians were told that the Bible was forbidden reading. While many provocative books have been written and published about Italians, this one deals with perhaps the most confrontational and sensitive subject one dare bring to the printed page...the religion of Italians! The labor of bringing this book to you is nothing less than a "herculean task," as Fratti puts it – "An important book that we must read with a healthy curiosity!"

David Mercaldo's Books

David Mercaldo's books can be ordered from Amazon.com or ask for them at Barnes and Noble or your favorite bookstore. A description of his current works is included at the end of this book.

A word from the Publisher

The word 'scripture' carries weight in any language. Historically it has been assigned only to documents that societies deemed "very important" – significant documents that guide and instruct in all manner of behaviors and actions. It is not surprising that key operational documents are dubbed, "The Bible" of this or that discipline. There are "golf bibles and even a "plumber's bible." In every case, they are thought to be definitive and complete! But there are other kinds of bibles bearing 'scriptures' that actually direct adherents to do away with anyone who doesn't agree with them. Other, so called 'scriptures,' engage followers to perform all kinds of emotional and mental acrobatics to achieve some higher state. Still, other documents describe mystical places beyond, outside, below or above our world. Not surprisingly, most create their own basis for authority that simply cannot be substantiated or corroborated. These are based on one person's vision, the ever-evolving dogma of an institution, or some mysterious document with no verifiable origin.

And then there are jocular systems that mock the entire concept, like Dadaism and the Church of Bob. They have their own "bibles," but they're just not Holy!

Sitting outside this cluster of confusion sits the Bible! Say what you will, it simply rises above the confusion in terms of scope, accuracy, consistency, and message. You may not choose to follow its teaching nor its answer for eternal salvation but any honest inquirer and student would have to admit that it is unique among religious documents.

Yet, even it has been maligned and encumbered with messages that distort its clarity and truth or the demand that someone other than the inquisitive individual interpret its "real" meaning.

That is the message of David Mercaldo's book... "The Other Italians." It is a provocative look at a religious system that has governed much of Italian life for millenniums, and how many are now realizing the simple message of the Gospel has been obscured by centuries of distortion. Playwright and theater critic, Mario Fratti, called it "an important book" and we agree!

So, read on! Read carefully! Read with an open mind...or shall I say an, "open heart!"

Marco Ciavolino, President - Paperclip Press

Preface

"Religion...the opium of the people!" We usually credit this excerpt to the German economist, Karl Marx, but in most references we are deprived of the complete quotation: "Religion is the sigh of the oppressed creature, the heart of a heartless world, and the soul of soulless conditions. It is the opium of the people." One has to wonder if Marx got his inspiration for this idea from the Marquis de Sade who first composed the phrase: "This opium you feed your people!" (1797) So what's an opiate? It's something that induces inaction and quiets uneasiness. Throughout history, heretical governments have probably been assisted more by religion and religious leaders - than artillery. It is not that religious leaders aligned themselves with despots and tyrants (some did), but the neglect of the church to intercede on behalf of the oppressed. But then again, that's another book!

In compliance with Mr. Marx's statement, it appears that since the beginning of time humans have sought the solace of spiritual and divine realms through organized, formal and informal religion, creed, tradition, culture and even occult practices. Reaching into the vast unknown realms of the sky, the earth and beneath, they called him or her by many names, and worshipped the same in a variety of ways.

Historic primitive carvings, various art forms and legend are not the only proof of this quest. The Biblical picture given to us by the Psalmist David adequately describes the surroundings that motivated this pursuit: *"The heavens are telling of the glory of God; and their expanse is declaring the work of His hands. Day to day pours forth speech, and night to night reveals knowledge. There is no speech, nor are there words; their voice is not heard. Their line has gone out through all the earth, and their utterances to the end of the world. In them He has placed a tent for the sun…"* (Psalms 19:1-4)

Out there in the great unknown is someone or something that people desire to embrace perceptually, emotionally and spiritually. They want to feel something; they want to do something! In some ways religion is indeed an opiate as it provides a kind of arousing stimulation along with psychological comfort. Religious affiliation tends to bind people together in a common cause and gives them an identity…personal and communal.

While most of the time men and women adhere to the religious practices of their parents or ethnic group, they are not short of other choices. Today, individuals can align themselves with religions that require more or less stringent qualifications and practices - including those that are permissive and tolerant of the vilest and most depraved human behavior. The latter are known as cults. Predictably religious affiliation and *psycho-spiritual* attachment for the individual or group appears to fluctuate with a variety of factors including: economics, personal and domestic problems, poverty, cultural trends, political oppression, and educational level – to mention just a few. There is even the occurrence where an entire civilization embraces a specific mystical belief or religion. Case in point…the Greeks!

In ancient times the Greeks worshipped and celebrated hundreds of gods. They named them, and ascribed certain meaning and characteristics to each. Historical records indicate they even sculptured and labeled one: *"The Unknown God."* (I humorously imagine they wanted to cover all bases just in case they overlooked and offended one). The record found in the New Testament - chronicled in the book of Acts describes how St. Paul the Apostle, dealt with the Greeks and their pursuit of an "unknown god." Specifically, he addresses, the men of Athens: *"So Paul stood in the midst of the Areopagus and said, Men of Athens, I observe that you are very religious in all respects. For while I was passing through and examining the objects of your worship, I also found an altar with this inscription, 'TO AN UNKNOWN GOD.' Therefore what you worship in ignorance, this I proclaim to you. The God who made the world and all things in it, since He is Lord of heaven and earth, does not dwell in temples made with hands; nor is He served by human hands, as though He needed anything, since He Himself gives to all people life and breath and all things; and He made from one man every nation of mankind to live on all the face of the earth, having determined their appointed times and the boundaries of their habitat ion, that they would seek God, if perhaps they might grope for Him and find Him, though He is not far from each one of us; for in Him we live and move and exist, as even some of your own poets have said, 'For we also are His children.' Being then the children of God, we ought not to think that the Divine Nature is like gold or silver or stone, an image formed by the art and thought of man. Therefore having overlooked the times of ignorance, God is now declaring to men that all people everywhere should repent"* (Acts17: 22-30)

Recent findings in the fields of architecture, science, art, and others substantiate that people living in the past did indeed embrace a diversity of sacred beliefs. The convictions and resultant practices attached to these revered values helped to define their own existence and the practices of their civilization. Along with their beliefs came ritual, ceremony and the necessity to fulfill certain "spiritual obligations." This is religion; and for those who embrace an organized or un-organized creed for that matter, the requirements are accepted, guarded and even enthusiastically defended with passionate and irrevocable conviction. There are even those who have died in their vow to defend and preserve these convictions. We know these people as, "Martyrs."

As mentioned, it is characteristic of people who embrace religion to feel an overwhelming need and even obligation to "do something" to attain favor and acceptance with congregants and their professed deity. This is often done in response and compliance to a written code for behavior.

An example of this kind of religious devotion and passion is seen in one of the largest religious communities in the world - with those who embrace the Roman Catholic Faith.

Roman Catholicism, having the world's most significant component of members, emanates from the first century, and constituents accept the dogma that it is the "True Church," carried forth with a succession of leaders originating with Peter, a Disciple of Jesus. It is a prime example of the need people have to do something or be something as membership in the Roman Catholic Church comes with a list of obligations, duties and expectations. It is a culture within a culture.

The question arises; if religion becomes an integral part of a culture, or culture an integral part of religion, has it lost its spiritual integrity, and will it not, over time embrace ideas and trends that are expedient for growth, and not rooted in its original dictates! That is to ask, if one is under the scrutiny and obligation of a religious community to act and perform in a lock-step manner, has it not become merely a socio-cultural ritual?

As with most religions, down through the centuries the Roman Catholic Church has been subject to external criticism and internal revolt because it veered from its original doctrinal beliefs.

It is important to review the historical path the Roman Catholic Church has taken to reach its present status in the world's religious clime. During its long history the Roman Catholic Church has enjoyed a committed membership of believers. But it has also experienced turmoil and dissention.

As early as 1350 AD there were attempts to reform the church from within…specifically by its clergy. At the onset of the sixteenth century, a Priest named Erasmus was among a group of other clergymen who called themselves, *Brethren of the Common Life*. Erasmus challenged the abusive powers of the Pope, Cardinals and Bishops. His focus was to bring them back to the purer days of the church by eliminating excessive, complicated ritual and dogma. He attempted to change the Church from within. Others from without also challenged the Church.

The Reformation, identified as, The Protestant Reformation, was not conducted by "Protestants." The name and group had not yet even come into existence. In fact, it was dissenting Priests within the Church who also sought to challenge basic acquired doctrines, the number of sacraments, and widespread corruption with the Church's leadership. These Priests initiated the reform movement. In fact, all of the Priest-reformers were born, baptized, confirmed and educated in the Roman Catholic Church.

For hundreds of years these Clerics spoke against the papacy, confession, purgatory, pilgrimages, worship of saints, relics, etc. It was a Monk, Roman Catholic Priest, and noted theologian by the name of Martin Luther who is best known as the leader of the movement. In reality, he followed a long line of those within the Church who witnessed the corrupted practices, and earnestly desired to bring about reform.

The essence of these challenges was based on a desire to return the Church to Biblical theology. Based on their understanding of the scriptures, the priest-reformers were convinced that the actions of the Roman Catholic Church did not resemble the church described in the New Testament.

When Roman Catholic Priest, Martin Luther read the scripture in Hebrews 10:38: *"But My righteous one shall live by faith;"* (Those who are justified shall live by faith) it propelled his thinking beyond the "religious" duties and requirements he had been taught to believe by his Church. Like the other Priests, it was never his intention to start a new religion! It was his hope to help bring about "reform."

In response to these Priest-dissenters, a Roman Catholic Counter Reformation ensued. *The Council of Trent* (1545–1563) attempted to re-establish the foundations of the Church. While most of Northern Europe was lost to Roman Catholicism, Southern Europe remained under its authority, and in other parts of the world Roman Catholicism continued to exist and grow.

In the 19th century the countries in Western Hemisphere became its target for growth. One group that ensured a populous for the Church in the new world, were those coming from Italy. By 1920 United States Italian immigrants numbered no less than four million. Today their numbers exceed seventeen million, and most of them are Roman Catholic.

During the past fifty years the Church's population has fluctuated around twenty-five percent largely in part to the immigration of Hispanics. But numbers don't tell the whole story about the Roman Catholic Church in America, and especially with that of its Italian members!

Something happened at the turn of the twentieth century that has indeed disrupted the continuity of their generational acceptance of the historic church. The western hemisphere, with its modernization, and ever-evolving scientific theories, has placed doubt in the minds of millions of Roman Catholics about what they are supposed to believe. This has resulted in a steady and continuous exodus with this and other ethnic groups! According to David E. Campbell and Robert D. Putnam in American Grace: How Religion Divides and Unites Us- *"...the Roman Catholic Church is hemorrhaging members."*

In an article published in *THE WEEK* (April 2010) the statistics were rolled out for review. *"It's the largest institutional crisis in centuries, possibly in church history," says the National Catholic Reporter. Worldwide, the Roman Catholic Church now has 1.1 billion members, compared with 1.5 billion Muslims and 593 million Protestants. In the U.S., all the major denominations have seen their numbers decline in recent years, but the Catholic Church has taken the biggest hit. Since the 1960s, four American-born Catholics have left the church for every one who has converted, according to a 2009 Pew study. In 2008 alone, Catholic membership declined by 400,000. More than 1,000 parishes have closed since 1995, and the number of priests has fallen from about 49,000 to 40,000 during that same period. Some 3,400 Catholic parishes in the U.S. now lack a resident priest. "Catholicism is in decline across America,"* says sociologist David Carlin.

What about in Europe? The situation there is even critical - especially in the most historically devout countries. In 1991, 84 percent of the Irish population attended Mass at least once a week. Today the weekly attendance figure is less than 50 percent. In Spain, 81 percent of the population identifies itself as Catholic, but two-thirds say they seldom or never attend services. And the priest shortage is acute—in England and Wales, the church ordained only 16 clergy members in all of 2009."

In 2012 the number of ordinations was 21. (CATHOLIC HERALD.co.uk May 5, 2014)

Current data indicates a continuing decline. Perhaps one way to explain their indifference and the resultant rejection in patronage is that we have entered a "secular age," where abortion, homosexuality, same-sex marriage, and tolerance for "individuality" (no matter what the behavior or rationale) has become accepted by Roman Catholics. This persists even though these are in conflict with the ordinances of their Church. Perhaps these open-minded or progressive members have succumbed to the "pick and choose" attitude that pervades most religions today.

With this trend has come a somewhat sinister attitude and even defiance of traditions and cultural expectations on many other fronts. Keep in mind the message of the 1960s to young people was to question authority! Given the freedom of this option to choose or reject religion, did Roman Catholic parents at that time actually believe it would not also corrupt the loyalty of their children and grandchildren to the church of their ancestry?

Some members of the Roman Catholic Church I surveyed were quick to blame a lack of effective educational practices in their Church as a cause for the movement of those who came of age in the latter part of the twentieth century. An indication of the lack of basic Roman Catholic beliefs showed itself with one of my survey questions: *Do you believe that during the Mass the bread and wine actually become the body and blood of Jesus?* The chapter that deals with TRANSUBSTANIATION reveals an astonishing response.

But the loss of members is not unique to the USA or Europe. Church members in South Africa, Asia, South America, Central America and the countries in the Caribbean are also questioning their beliefs and denouncing the historic faith of their parents. While there is growth in membership in some regions, the overall census is diminishing. Dutch Bishops, who recently visited the Pope, confessed over Vatican Radio that they are facing hundreds of church closures and an ongoing exodus of members. Willem Jacobus Eijk Cardinal, Archbishop of Utrecht and chairman of the Dutch Bishops' conference confessed, *"The Catholic Church in the Netherlands is facing a near collapse...the number of practicing Catholics is diminishing very quickly...in the 1950s, 90 percent of Catholics still went to church every Sunday. Now, it's only five percent!"* (LifeSite News-December 5, 2013)

With young people there are many and varied reasons for the exodus. During the last fifty years the world has produced what I call, *"media-bred children"* who see no efficacy in religion. Our colleges and universities...perhaps the entire public education arena has presented children of the twentieth century with a world-view that is in direct conflict with the teachings of the Roman Catholic Church. But this also includes many other denominations, religious cults and sects. Label it open-minded, progressive, liberal; today's young people do not hallow the historic doctrines, obligations and sacraments of their church. It is an age of choice, and they're not choosing religion.

Secularism is fast replacing Roman Catholic Church discipline with the "New Millennials" wanting little to do with anything "religious." They'll state they are *"spiritual,"* as long as it is understood they are not part of a formal religious body!

But this book is more about what really has replaced the formal religious practices of the Church in Rome and others, than the reasons found within its institutional structure or societal trends causing the defection of so many Italians. With that said, we will examine a singular identifiable factor that has entreated historically faithful Roman Catholic Italians to reconsider their devotion. The author calls this population, THE OTHER ITALIANS.

The result of extensive research has yielded the following: These Other Italians have embraced the Holy Scriptures, and call themselves, "Bible believing Christians." Interestingly, this movement is similar to the one that challenged the Church hundreds of years ago.

One might aptly call it a *"Back to the Bible movement…again!"*

This book is offered as an explanation for this phenomenon and every attempt has been made to present the content in as factual manner as possible. The information is framed for comparing, contrasting and explaining what members of the Roman Catholic Church and The Other Italians believe about selected topics and why they believe as they do.

One must keep in mind the label "Christian" encompasses many sects and divisions within the Christian religion emanating from New Testament times. Thus, the commitment of this author is not to argue the merits of one set of religious beliefs or doctrines over another. For the most part much of what is written herein is based on that which can be found in the Bible, and the testimony of *The Other Italians* you may know - those typical of the individuals the author interviewed during his research phase.

The text of these pages emanates from hundreds of consultations, questionnaires, surveys and extensive research garnered from commentaries, dictionaries, lexicons, numerous articles, editorials, encyclopedias, sermons, and homilies - most of which are readily available on the worldwide net. The information presented herein was not written as an argument against the teachings of the Roman Catholic Church, but primarily authored with the intention of clarifying what THE OTHER ITALIANS believe. It is written from the perspective of this unique group…it was not authored in defense of them, not for them but about them!

The NEW AMERICAN STANDARD BIBLE is primarily employed for references as it contains the canon of scriptures accepted by both the Roman Catholic Church and *The Other Italians.*

Who are the "Other Italians?"

There is a worldwide occurrence that is shaking the foundations of the Roman Catholic Church as countless members are challenging doctrines, questioning its authority and are defecting in record numbers. This does not seem to be based on the simple exchange of one set of ideas for another, but what appears to be, as some call it, a "spiritual awakening;" and not the advent of a new religion. The heart of this change is prompting people to accept the Bible as their only source for religious inspiration and teaching...thus rejecting the idea of a "Mother Church" as having equal authority with the Holy Scriptures.

To many of the faithful Italian adherents of Roman Catholicism, this is heresy - a blind and blasphemous abandonment of the *"True Church."* The question that is presented by those Italians who do hold fast to the instruction, mandates and traditions of the historic Church is this:

How can you be an Italian and not Roman Catholic?

The rejection and re-direction that is moving people away from the teachings of the Roman Catholic Church goes beyond the idea of an individual adopting an emotional or intellectual religious alternative. It encompasses something that has been seen at different times throughout history in different parts of the world. (*The Reformation in Europe was such a still point*).

The Other Italians confirm their decision is based on an uncompromising and unwavering acceptance of the Bible as the primary source for understanding an individual's relationship with God. So profound and threatening is this trend, that in the historical timeline of the Roman Catholic Church there is a period when reading the Bible was actually prohibited.

The contention or conviction is that an individual can have a direct, spiritual and *"personal"* relationship with God through His son, Jesus Christ, and that no earthly institution can initiate or govern this relationship.

The phenomenon has also affected people of other cultures and religion but more profoundly, with those in the Italian community. But exactly how did this change come about and why would Italians leave the Mother Church?

As the twentieth century emerged, millions of immigrants came to the Americas and brought with them their various traditions. Many of these were fashioned by generations of religious affiliation, devotion and teaching. Secular and cultural factors also entered into their new life on these distant shores. Sometimes there was an indistinguishable line separating what was initiated by an ever-evolving culture, and their religious practices…that were also evolving and altering historic rudimentary ideas and beliefs. But in spite of outside influences in many areas of their lives, there was a kind of loyalty that connected them to their past religious practices!

Evidence of this, for example, is seen in the affection Italians had, and continue to have for their PATRON SAINTS. Immigrants clung to both social-cultural and religious practices when they transitioned from Europe to the Americas. Today, a hundred plus years later and thousands of miles away, generations still worship and pay homage to their ancestral religious heroes with festivals, parades, and devotion. It continues to be part of their religious practices.

The adoption of patron saints finds its root in the middle ages. As organized cities emerged, a church official, perhaps a priest who lived in the area, was given a place of prominence. Saints often became the patrons of places where they were born or had been active in ministerial duties. Thus, the idea of patron saints grew out of religion, culture and tradition. One's patron saint became part of his or her devout observance and worship. Further, in many cases the patron saint was *canonized* which elevated their spiritual status (Canonization occurs when the Pope proclaims the person has been faithful to the Church, possesses laudable virtue, and can serve as an "intercessor"). Thus, they are accepted and worshipped as spiritual emissaries that could go to God on the behalf of the faithful.

Those coming from Italy and Sicily were no exception! While most were unable to pack more than a duffle bag of belongings, they did take something else. They packed their religion, Roman Catholicism, along with the memory of their patron saints! These immigrants were determined to honor and worship them in their new home. Surely, this would anchor them to their families, and the beloved traditions they celebrated in the old country - as well as continuing with the practices of the only religious theology they had ever known.

Moving to all parts of the country, the various European immigrant groups mingled, which consequentially fostered an integration of cultures and traditions. But in spite of this assimilation, for nearly a hundred years, most people stayed within their own religious and national community, continuing the historic cultural and religious practices of their ancestors. Southern and Northern and Western Europeans felt kindred to each other if their religious faith was wrapped in Roman Catholicism, with its orthodox traditions and servitude.

However, during the past hundred years, something happened to many Italians! They came in contact with individuals who were, "Bible Believing Christians" of various faiths (*Baptist, Holiness, Church of God, Pentecostal, Assemblies of God, etc.*). As a result, these same Italians began reading the Bible, and hearing the preaching of the Gospel of Salvation through faith alone.

Following this initial contact, *The Other Italians* learned from the Holy Scriptures that their eternal destiny was not reliant on being a member of an institutional church. They embraced what they read in the Bible and heard in sermons about the "Grace of God" to save them and give them eternal life.

The message of achieving salvation through God's grace alone was not taught by the historic Church. The idea stood in stark contrast to the religious dogma Italians had been taught to believe, where obedience to the Church was the only pathway by which a person could achieve salvation.

One scripture, among many (written by the Apostle Paul to the Church in Ephesus), challenged the ideas that anyone or any institution controlled an individual's salvation and ultimate eternal fate. Here is his disclosure to the members of the Church in Ephesus: *"For by grace you have been saved through faith; and that not of yourselves, it is the gift of God; not as a result of works, so that no one may boast."* (Ephesians 2:8-9

The Other Italians read and believed that personal salvation came through faith alone, and that it is not predicated on being "good" or doing nice things for others, although that is a part of the Christian ministry. They began to reject the idea that organized or unorganized religion was the only option they had in their desire to know God.

Members of the Roman Catholic Church are taught through homily, baptism, confirmation, catechism, and celebration of the Mass, that loyalty and obedience to the Church, and doing good works, was the determinant in their going to heaven or hell when they died. They are taught that the Church controls their ultimate destiny. *The Other Italians* believe these ideas are in conflict with the Holy Bible that speaks of God's sustaining grace and personal faith.

Historically, while many church congregations sprung up as recorded in the New Testament, no one church was given any extra authority or prominence. As these *Other Italians* read the scriptures, they came to discern and accept the premise that their own unique salvation lay in the life, death and resurrection of Jesus Christ...and nothing else. Consequently, these Italians placed their faith solely in Jesus and rejected the idea that the Roman Catholic Church was the *"True Church"* of the New Testament. In doing so, they have become known to many of their family members and friends as, *"The Other Italians."*

As already stated, the purpose of this book is to publish the reasons why Italians have left the Roman Catholic Church, and embraced the teachings of the Bible as their source of inspiration and spiritual direction. The book will site the scriptures that *The Other Italians* believe, and affirm, how God's grace is extended to mankind. The content will focus on specific scriptures that answer two important questions:

What is the means of salvation?

What is the New Testament Church?

Today, *the Other Italians* eagerly identify the specific scriptures that have directed and nurtured their movement away from the historic Roman Catholic Church and other religions. As you read this book, it is important to keep in mind that they are *"Bible Believing Christians,"* depending solely on the scriptures, and holding no allegiance or ties to any organized religion - although many do worship in Baptist, Methodist, Presbyterian and other churches. They do not accept the premise that membership and adherence to any set of rules or edicts is a means or way of salvation. Their attendance at a church service is solely for the purpose of fellowshipping with others that believe as they do, and to learn from the scriptures. They are under no obligation to attend a physical church except to adhere to the scriptures that admonish believers not to forsake assembling together.

The Other Italians have chosen to embrace something less tangible than the great gothic structures or the mystery of symbols and ceremony. They exercise a very simple, and yet compelling faith. This confidence has them accepting and believing only the scriptures. This has historically been known as, "Solo Scriptura" (*The scriptures only*).

They recognize the New Testament Church as a fellowship of all like-minded people (*believers*), and totally reject the idea that any institution can claim sovereignty or control in matters of their salvation and eternal destiny.

While there are similarities between Roman Catholicism and Bible Believing Christians, there are also grave differences that are, for the most part, irreconcilable. These irreconcilable differences are the main thread upon which this book is based, and topics have been carefully chosen, not for the purpose of debate, but rather to contrast and compare the beliefs.

Written topically, it is the intention of this book to answer questions relating to *The Other Italian*!

To begin, they call themselves: "*Born again Christians*!"

Chapter One: What it means to be a "Born Again" Christian

The Other Italians readily identify themselves as "Born Again Christians." Now, you might think this label is a designation for a new "religion." It is not! As already stated these Italian, "Born-Againers" are not aligned with any institutional church, organized denomination or religious body.

Another label you might hear among this group is the word, "SAVED." It is not uncommon to hear *The Other Italians* say that they got "saved," and can point to a day and time of their *conversion* or what some like to call, *completion.* Words and expressions like these have a variety of meanings and inferences: (*believer, born anew, a spiritual new birth, and regeneration, to mention just a few*). One member of this community remarked that in the past he had Jesus on his mind, but not in his heart. *"It's an eighteen inch difference; you move a consciousness of Jesus from the head to the heart; that makes all the difference!*

So where did these terms or labels really come from; who coined them; when were they first used and given meaning?

When I interview people about the subject, there seems to be a misconception that the term, "Born Again," is associated with a *religious trend* of the twentieth century. This is not the case! To find the first use of these words, we must examine the Holy Scriptures and focus on an event in the life of Jesus as recorded in the book of Saint John. There we will see…

The first recorded use of the words *"Born Again"* was by none other than Jesus!

Jesus uttered these words over two thousand years ago! I imagine you might be quite surprised to hear this; yet it is indeed a fact! When I questioned my Roman Catholic interviewees about the origin of this term only a few ascribed it to Jesus. Most were surprised. Some even denied it; at which time I opened to the passage where they read it for themselves.

In the particular portion of the scriptures below, we find Jesus informing an inquisitive religious leader that he must be "born again." The account is found in the book of Saint John 3: 1-20. (The Bible is sectioned by book, chapter and verse. Scripture quotes from the Bible used in this book will be referenced accordingly). Here's the text! *"Now there was a man of the Pharisees, named Nicodemus, a ruler of the Jews; this man came to Jesus by night and said to Him, "Rabbi, we know that You have come from God as a teacher; for no one can do these signs that You do unless God is with him." Jesus answered and said to him, "Truly, truly, I say to you, unless one is born again he cannot see the kingdom of God. Nicodemus said to Him, "How can a man be born when he is old? He cannot enter a second time into his mother's womb and be born, can he?" Jesus answered, "Truly, truly, I say to you, unless one is born of water and the Spirit he cannot enter into the kingdom of God. That which is born of the flesh is flesh, and that which is born of the Spirit is spirit. Do not be amazed that I said to you, 'You must be born again.' The wind blows where it wishes and you hear the sound of it, but do not know where it comes from and where it is going; so is everyone who is born of the Spirit."*

Nicodemus said to Him, "How can these things be?" Jesus answered and said to him, "Are you the teacher of Israel and do not understand these things? Truly, truly, I say to you, we speak of what we know and testify of what we have seen, and you do not accept our testimony. If I told you earthly things and you do not believe, how will you believe if I tell you heavenly things? No one has ascended into heaven, but He who descended from heaven: the Son of Man. As Moses lifted up the serpent in the wilderness, even so must the Son of Man be lifted up; so that whoever believes will in Him have eternal life.

*For God so loved the world that He gave His only begotten Son, that who-
ever believes in Him shall not perish, but have eternal life. For God did not send
the Son into the world to judge the world, but that the world might be saved
through Him. He who believes in Him is not judged; he who does not believe
has been judged already, because he has not believed in the name of the only
begotten Son of God. This is the judgment, that the Light has come into the
world, and men loved the darkness rather than the Light, for their deeds were
evil. For everyone who does evil hates the Light, and does not come to the Light
for fear that his deeds will be exposed. But he who practices the truth comes to
the Light, so that his deeds may be manifested as having been wrought in God."*
As you can see the words "Born Again" were not coined by an individual or
group! They are the words of Jesus!

The question to be answered now is a simple one: What did Jesus mean
when he used these words in answer to Nicodemus's inquiry about his identity?

To begin, Jesus tells Nicodemus, *"I say to you, unless one is born again,
he cannot "SEE" the kingdom of God."* This religious leader came to visit Jesus
during the evening hours. Prior to his visit Nicodemus appears to have already determined there was something religious about Jesus and identifies
Him as someone associated with God. *("Rabbi, we know that You have come
from God as a teacher; for no one can do these signs that You do unless God is
with him).*

You would expect Jesus to respond to this statement by confirming its
accuracy. But he doesn't! In response He says that in order to "SEE" the
Kingdom of God, Nicodemus must be "born again." In essence he tells his
questioner that he could guess all night long as to His identity, but could
not truly know who He is unless he had a unique experience. Only then
would he be able to discern Jesus' true identity. This *experience* would even
transcend his best intellectual thinking!

Actually, Jesus was saying, *"Nicodemus, you've got to be born again to
know who I am!"* Another meaning of the expression, *born again*, comes
from the Greek and defines it - *"to be begotten from above or having been born
from above." (The word "Begotten" means to be created, as in something new, a*

new creation). Jesus was proposing that Nicodemus needed a new kind of *birth* in order to recognize who He is.

Let's take a closer look at this passage of scripture. To begin with, what wasn't this religious leader SEEING? Keep in mind that this is a Jew, questioning a Jew, and while Nicodemus was a *student* of the law, Jesus *authored* it! He knew the law, but didn't *recognize*, or shall we say, SEE the author!

Jesus looks at his visitor and tells him that in order to *"see,"* (to know Him, and what He's is all about), he would have to experience something that he had never been taught about in all the years of his religious education, and service as a religious leader in the Jewish community. Nicodemus would have to experience something in order to enter a realm of understanding not familiar to him. Jesus uses the words, "Born again" as the gateway to this understanding. Nicodemus is obviously confused! *"Born again?"* Jesus confirms that humans give earthly life. Surely Nicodemus had no problem understanding this.

Then Jesus explains, while humans produce an *earthly* birth, the *(Holy) Spirit* produces a *spiritual* birth. This was news! Jesus then informs him that he would not experience a *spiritual* birth until he realized his spiritual condition.

The Other Italians confess that at one time, like Nicodemus, they too were spiritually blind. *Spiritual birth* can be described as REGENERATION. In the field of biology, regeneration is the process of renewal, restoration, and growth. It is the same with the spiritual being…these are the same processes of renewal, restoration and growth.

This *regeneration* would not be physical or intellectual but spiritual. Nicodemus intellectually identifies Jesus as *"someone come from God."* But one cannot know who Jesus really is until he or she experiences a regenerative *spiritual* birth. (*The Other Italians* conclude that Nicodemus line of questioning indicates his *spiritual eyes* had not yet opened!).

The Apostle Paul wrote a letter to the Church in Ephesus and reminded them that at one time they were "dead" in their sins but by Christ Jesus they were made to be alive! *"And you were dead in your trespasses an sin."*(Ephesians 2:1) The good news is given when Jesus informs Nicodemus he could come alive *spiritually*. But this necessitated something: Nicodemus had to experience this regeneration…a renewal, revival - a divine re-birth. He could be "reborn spiritually, but the moment he was dead in his sin! Note, He doesn't tell his questioner about a church or church leaders who can serve as intermediaries between him and God. He doesn't spell out a list of requirements, nor does he offer an artifact or relic. He doesn't speak of a "temporary fix." Jesus offers Himself to Nicodemus! *You can know me…here's how!* He was not only offering himself as a physical being, but a redeemer! And the relationship would be permanent! The irony of this offer is that nothing was required of Nicodemus. He just had to acknowledge and accept the offer Jesus was making. This was something far more personal than association with a church or organization.

What Nicodemus had to experience was a *spiritual transformation of the heart;* then his ability to *see* the kingdom would be reality. He would move from the point or position of questioning who Jesus was, to a total understanding of who He is! But something was missing in this religious man's life…something that blocked him from really *seeing* and understanding the things of God, transparent and personal. But what was inhibiting his spiritual insight? Here is the truth that *The Other Italians* speak about when they share the details of their new life in Christ Jesus. Nicodemus had to recognize his deficiency.

As with all people…his deficiency is *sin,* and sin was separating him from a relationship with God. He was dead in his sin…that is he was spiritually dead! *"And you were dead in your trespasses and sins."* (Ephesians 2:1) Like *The Other Italians,* Nicodemus had to repent of his sin. God's Holy Spirit cannot dwell in someone who is in this un-regenerated state and only the Holy Spirit can open an individual's eyes to comprehend the person of Jesus. To *see* and know Jesus…the sin has to go!

The Apostle St. Paul put it this way in his writings to the church in Rome. Here is an all-inclusive statement found in St. Paul's message to the Romans. It just might be among the most important scriptures in the Bible. *"For all have sinned, and fall short of the glory of God!"* (Romans 3:23) Nicodemus would have to do some serious thinking! Like *The Other Italians* of today, he had to recognize his "un-regenerated state," and confess that he was a sinner. All of his thoughts about being righteous because he kept the law to the best of his ability had to go. The ritual, pretentious piety, and all that goes with religion had to be removed and replaced. The Bible says: *"that if you confess with your mouth Jesus as Lord, and believe in your heart that God raised Him from the dead, you will be saved;"* (Romans 10:9)

Salvation is of the heart! The heart believes, the mouth professes. But this is more than a verbal profession of faith in Jesus. Many people in the Christian community verbally profess their "Christianity," but have not experienced the new birth. A confession has no value unless there is repentance. Note - Jesus does not offer a certain prayer, or a specific statement…but rather an opening of the mind and HEART. *The Other Italians* told me that while Biblical passages a person might recite from memory (i.e. *"The Lord's Prayer"*) can focus their mind for a few moments and give them a *religious feeling* it remains a kind of emotional prose, and has no bearing on a real relationship with God.

In an interview, one older Italian gentleman related to me that shortly after he arrived in Manhattan he met an Italian couple from his hometown in Italy who shared the message of faith with him. He accepted Christ as his Savior, and came to know Jesus in a personal and intimate way. He shared a story with me when I told him about this chapter. *"There was great actor who was known to end his theatrical run by going out to the audience and reciting the Twenty-third Psalm ("The Lord is my Shepherd…"). One night he lost his voice, and the stage crews suggested the curtain man recite it for him to help continue the tradition. The popular actor walked to the center stage and stood next to the humble man and listened as he recited the entire chapter. It was no great oration, but a deep heartfelt and emotionally moving recitation of the familiar scripture passage. Something was special about his recitation. When he was finished, there was no applause. The audience sat in awe and was silent until one patron stood to his feet and started a singular applause. Seconds later the entire audience stood and applauded for several minutes. While the actor often enjoyed a standing ovation, it was nothing compared what he witnessed that evening. When the room again became silent, the actor put his arm around the man, looked out into the audience and spoke. The difference between this man and me is that I know the Psalm, but he obviously knows the SHEP-HERD!"*

In their former state, *The Other Italians* were religious, sounded religious, and like most people tried to live a good "religious life." They knew the Psalm! Some were very involved in their church and known in their community for their devotion. Many even had a reputation in their community as being "spiritual." But they came to realize that good behavior, although admirable, did little to bring them to a point of the *spiritual rebirth* they learned about from the scriptures, the one that Nicodemus was confronted with that night when he visited Jesus. For years they professed their religious affiliation, but not their *faith,* and did not have any kind of assurance of forgiveness before God. You might say they were righteous before people, but not God! They knew the Psalm, but not the Shepherd!

The Disciple St. Matthew wrote: *"Not everyone who says to Me, 'Lord, Lord,' will enter the kingdom of heaven, but he who does the will of My Father who is in heaven will enter."* (Matthew 7:21)

The Other Italians know that an individual is not saved by reciting some enchanting words or by performing certain religious rites or rituals. There is no magic involved nor is there a mystical or even alleged supernatural *incantation* to enjoin a person to the Lord Jesus. He understands English and all languages spoken on the earth. He is quite familiar with a *sinner's prayer!*

The Scriptures are clear! Salvation starts with the recognition of our sinful state, followed by a profession of faith in Christ Jesus. St. John tells us what God's will is concerning salvation—to BELIEVE on His son, Jesus! *"For this is the will of My Father, that everyone who beholds the Son and believes in Him will have eternal life, and I Myself will raise him up on the last day."* St. John 6:40

This is an important "look," and means more than just gazing. It *denotes beholding, accepting* and finally *embracing.* Many people look, but fail to embrace and truly believe. Cerebral or mental agreement to the truths of God is insufficient! Something has to follow and it is explained in Hebrews 11:6:

"And without faith it is impossible to please Him, for he who comes to God must believe that He is and that He is a rewarder of those who seek Him."

The Apostle Paul wrote this in a letter to the church in Ephesus: *"For by grace you have been saved through faith; and that not of yourselves, it is the gift of God; not as a result of works, so that no one may boast."* (Ephesians 2:8) Here is it is in a nutshell! Saving grace is a gift of God! You receive it by simply believing (exercising faith). And you can't do anything to merit or earn it...no matter how good you think you are!

You probably remember the story of *"Doubting Thomas the Disciple."* Here's my abbreviated version. After the resurrection, Jesus appears to his Disciples. Thomas is not in attendance. The others go and tell Thomas that they've seen the Lord. Thomas announces, *"Unless I see the nail marks in his hands and put my finger where the nails were, and put my hand into his side, I will not believe."* A week later the group is assembled again and the Lord makes an appearance. Thomas was in for a shock because right off he recognizes the Savior. Jesus tells him, *"Put your finger here; see my hands. Reach out your hand and put it into my side. Stop doubting and believe."*

Like Thomas, *The Other Italians* told me they first had to overcome their doubt by opening up their mind and heart to accept the simple, uncomplicated message of salvation by faith alone. Jesus put it this way to Thomas: *"Blessed are those who have not seen and yet have believed."* The scriptures continue to remind *The Other Italians* to bind (to attach or connect) in their heart the provisions of the new birth in Christ Jesus. Consider these promises: Jeremiah 29:11-13: *"For I know the plans that I have for you,' declares the Lord, 'plans for welfare and not for calamity to give you a future and a hope. Then you will call upon Me and come and pray to Me, and I will listen to you. You will seek Me and find Me when you search for Me with all your heart.*

Psalm 91: *"He who dwells in the shelter of the Most High will abide in the shadow of the Almighty. I will say to the Lord, "My refuge and my fortress, My God, in whom I trust!"*

Psalm 27:13-14: *"I would have despaired unless I had believed that I would see the goodness of the Lord in the land of the living. Wait for the Lord; be strong and let your heart take courage; Yes, wait for the Lord.'* (The message here is be confident in your trust of the Lord)

Proverbs 3:5-7: *"Trust in the Lord with all your heart and do not lean on your own understanding. In all your ways acknowledge Him, and He will make your paths straight. Do not be wise in your own eyes. Fear the Lord and turn away from evil."*

Note these scriptures are found in the Old Testament. Perhaps Nicodemus had read them, yet he had never "seen" them!

SAVED BY GRACE - THROUGH FAITH!

In the book of Hebrews the writer reminds the congregation: *"The just shall live by faith!"* This verse is found in chapter 10, and verse 28. It has prompted people throughout the ages to reconsider the pathway to God, and question any individual or religious institution that says there is another way! It is an all-inclusive verse, pairs itself with no other, and leaves no further option on the table for salvation.

Jesus told Nicodemus that he needed a new kind of thinking - one that would open up his mind and heart to God by the power of the Holy Spirit. When that *surrender* occurs, then he would have 20/20 *spiritual vision*. But he needed a new foundation to build upon, not just a fix up of the old person. When our physical birth occurs we begin life with a clean slate. When our spiritual birth occurs we are washed clean, totally forgiven and we can build a new life with Jesus as Lord.

The Other Italians say that the new birth brings about new thinking! The accountability of who we are and what we do is to Him and no one else. Nicodemus had to undergo a total change: a new nature, new affections and new aims. It is to be born to a life of communion with God, and would result in a continuous consciousness of Him. Again, this was not an intellectual awakening but a *spiritual* one. It would emerge when he experienced the "second birth" Jesus told him about.

The Other Italians, like the inquisitive Pharisee Nicodemus, heard they could actually partake of a *divine spiritual nature*. It didn't mean they'd walk around with a halo on their heads, but now possessed an inheritance of knowledge through reading the Word of God, and having Jesus Christ dwelling "within them." Christ imparts wisdom *within* an individual, which helps them to make the right choices resulting in a life free from the guilt of sin, and separation from God. The stress of guilt can destroy mentally, emotionally, socially, and ultimately physically!

The Other Italians told me their life with its familiar surroundings, problems, trials did not disappear; but they now had Christ Jesus living in them. While their ancestors looked above to the heavens for the divine and spiritual, Jesus came to live 'within.'

Listen to the message of two prophets: *Jeremiah* and *Ezekiel* who foretold the Holy Spirit would dwell *within* the individual. In the Old Testament we read that the Children of Israel had the Law of God on physical earthen tablets. These prophets foretold of a time when the Law of God would be written, not on tablets, but in the hearts of men! While God chose Moses to deliver the Law to the people, the Holy Spirit is now the one to reveal the mind of God to man by indwelling (within) them. *"Behold, days are coming," declares the Lord, "when I will make a new covenant with the house of Israel and with the house of Judah, not like the covenant which I made with their fathers in the day I took them by the hand to bring them out of the land of Egypt, My covenant which they broke, although I was a husband to them," declares the Lord. "But this is the covenant which I will make with the house of Israel after those days," declares the Lord, "I will put My law within them and on their heart I will write it; and I will be their God, and they shall be My people. They will not teach again, each man his neighbor and each man his brother, saying, 'Know the Lord,' for they will all know Me, from the least of them to the greatest of them," declares the Lord, "for I will forgive their iniquity, and their sin I will remember no more."(Jeremiah 31)*

The Other Italians say they are assured of the presence of God in their heart, and with such, they have the confidence and wisdom to deal intelligently with each situation in their life. I did not meet one convert who claimed to have a perfect life, nor did they propose that one is not subject to pressures and disappointments. The difference was in how they handled each situation.

This is what being *born again* is all about! This is the difference between being religious and being *regenerated* by the power of the Holy Spirit within. In St. John 14:17 we read, *"that is the Spirit of truth, whom the world cannot receive, because it does not SEE Him or know Him, but you know Him because He abides with you and will be in you.* God's Holy Spirit dwells within the individual who is regenerated.

One of my interviewees stated: *"Religion puts a new coat ON the man, while Jesus puts a new man IN the coat!"* Keep in mind Jesus' questioner was a religious leader. Organized religions up to his time period in history codified its expectations. One was not told he or she could not know God in a personal way. That was thought to be impossible, even blasphemous. God was up there in the sky far removed and away from them. The average person had to adhere to certain beliefs and act according to specific *religious expectations and even mandates.* He or she had to follow rules to fulfill religious duties authored by men who were under the impression one must do something to achieve God's acceptance. Such thinking eradicates the message of the Gospel that assures the person of God's never-ending grace to save and keep them! Once again, here's St. Paul's letter to the congregation in Ephesus: *"For by grace you have been saved through faith; and that not of yourselves, it is the gift of God; not as a result of works, so that no one may boast.* (Ephesians 2:8-9)

Throughout history religion has done more to enslave than liberate! It is a proven tool that many have used to control the mind and heart of the masses. An example of this occurred in 1978 when over nine hundred people died as a result of this kind of *mind management* in the name of "religion" at the hands of a leader named Jim Jones in Jonestown, Guyana. Jesus had nothing to do with this tragedy…religion did it!

Jesus looked at Nicodemus and informed him that he must experience a *transformation*, one that would move him from having a self-serving nature to one of righteousness and holiness. Again, this was unheard of in the *religious world* of his day.

In consideration of the text in this chapter I thought if ever there was a point in Jesus' ministry when and where He could establish a "religion" it was that recorded night with the man, Nicodemus. He might have used this situation to announce the creation of a new physical church to be organized by him. Jesus could have easily enumerated requirements, expectations and all that goes with organizing a system for a religion. But he did not! What Nicodemus had to do was accept God's standards and his ways for his life. *The Other Italians* recognize their need for this spiritual re-birth...a direct connection to heaven through a relationship with Jesus. Some Biblical scholars, using the Greek and Hebrew, interpret "Born Again" to mean *"Born from above."*

Consider the contrast...one birth by earth and the other by heaven...one a *physical* birth, and the other a *spiritual* one.

Again, Nicodemus, like most, responds to Jesus' message of being "born again," or being spiritually reborn, in human terms. He thinks of this birth process as a human function. *"Hey, I was already born; what is this "born again" thing all about? How can this be?"* In response, Jesus extends his message by adding, *"Except a man be born of water and of Spirit, he cannot enter the Kingdom of God."* First we heard one must be born again to SEE; now Jesus says he could actually ENTER the kingdom.

As with any anticipated destination, we can usually see it coming into view *("See the Kingdom of God")* - upon arrival it is then possible to enter it *("Enter the Kingdom")*. Nicodemus had already experienced a physical birth; Jesus says now he must experience a heavenly birth by being *born of water and of the Spirit*. Again, the message can be summed in that one word: RE-GENERATION. Nicodemus' soul had to be regenerated, renewed, *born anew!* Jesus says, *"being born of water!"* Based on a totality of scriptures *The Other Italians* know that the act of water baptism does not have the power to save them, or bring them into the Kingdom of Heaven; so the reference to "water" is not connected to baptism.

The Bible is our record that many of those Jesus brought into the Kingdom were never *baptized* in water. Actually, there is no record in the Bible that Jesus ever baptized anyone in water.

Jesus' mission on earth was to seek and save those who were lost. We read that in Dr. Luke's Gospel (Yes, he was a physician)- Luke 19:10:

"For the Son of Man has come to seek and to save that which was lost." He did not use any rite or ceremony in His ministry to bring salvation to mankind. If He did, the natural inclination would have been to cling to something tangible, thereby corrupting and thwarting His ministry. Based on the scriptures, *The Other Italians* believe, to come into the kingdom, the individual man or woman must exercise *faith alone* and not rely upon some personal action.

I've already identified the basic nature of people to want to do something to attain something, even in their religious eagerness. An example of what people believe they must do to receive God's forgiving grace is to be baptized. *The Other Italians* know that water baptism has never saved anyone. Water baptism is a testimony to others that they have accepted Jesus as their Savior.

In other words, it shows what has already happened in the life of a believer (the new birth). *The Other Italians* do not believe *water baptism* saves a person. The word "water" in this verse is used *figuratively* as a sense of salvation of *"being washed clean,"* and His use of the words, *"Born of the Spirit,"* mean to be *"born again."*

Throughout the Bible, Jesus is referred to as the "Living Word." *The Other Italians* now "SEE" the Kingdom because they understand that sin separates them from God, and they have confessed their sin. They not only confessed, but also repented of their sin. This conversion finds the individual in *spiritual surrender* to God, not to a church or creed or religion. They understand and accept the Bible that declares Jesus is this *Living Word.* Thus, the Bible becomes the chief source of teaching, and learning about the new Kingdom they have ENTERED into as a result of being "born from above."

The Other Italians do not go to Jesus with a long list of the sins they have committed in their life and ask for forgiveness. No one is capable of listing every single sin they've ever committed. What they confessed to God was their sinful nature…unbridled and uncontrolled by the Holy Spirit! In the words of noted theologian, John Calvin we see the inescapable consequence of who we are as a fallen race - *"We aren't sinners because we sin, we sin because we're sinners!"*

One interviewee spoke to me about the obvious parallel that describes their journey, *"When I was born, I had a lot of growing to do. It is the same with being re-born from above. I also had a lot of growing to do. That came by reading the Word of God! My own faith increases as I heard the Word of God preached."* The Other Italians are not waiting to die so they can ENTER the Kingdom of God.

"You enter the kingdom when the Holy Spirit takes up residency in your heart; it's an inside happening," another offered.

The Other Italians understand that being born again is the key to the kingdom that Jesus spoke about. One who knows the way of salvation holds the key. Did not Jesus command His disciples to *"go ye therefore into all the world and preach the gospel?"* He said they had the *keys to the kingdom.* The key to heaven is the new birth!

SO WHAT ABOUT HEAVEN?

Jesus laid out the plan for inheriting "eternal life" with just five words: *"YOU MUST BE BORN AGAIN!"* The Other Italians confirmed that there is no record of Jesus ever saying one could enter the Kingdom by doing good works or being good. They question that if being "good," and performing good works could get you into heaven, why did Jesus come to earth? What would be the point of His life, death and resurrection? The "good works" argument to get to heaven is not substantiated by any scripture in the Bible…cover to cover! However, the demonstration of a new life in Christ is manifested in service to others!

These *Other Italians* declared they have no antagonism against the Church of their youth. The cultural ties to the Italian community, and its many organizations are still part of their life. However, they have accepted the invitation Jesus offered to Nicodemus in verse 16 and 17: *"For God so loved the world, that He gave His only begotten Son, that whoever believes in Him shall not perish, but have eternal life. For God did not send the Son into the world to judge the world, but that the world might be saved through Him."*

In summary, The Other Italians believe salvation comes directly from God, through the sacrificial death of Jesus on the cross. He alone took their sins and the sins of the whole world. This was the ultimate sacrifice demanded by God to redeem mankind back to a state of fellowship with Him.

St. John wrote: *"but if we walk in the Light as He Himself is in the Light, we have fellowship with one another, and the blood of Jesus His Son cleanses us from all sin."* (1 John 1:7) They have accepted Jesus as the one and only means of salvation. He is their Savior and they do not accept any other ways or means to attain salvation from their sinful, un-regenerated state.

As for the religious leader, Nicodemus; Saint John wrote about him once again at the time of Jesus' death: *"After these things Joseph of Arimathea, being a disciple of Jesus, but a secret one for fear of the Jews, asked Pilate that he might take away the body of Jesus; and Pilate granted permission. So he came and took away His body. Nicodemus, who had first come to Him by night, also came, bringing a mixture of myrrh and aloes, about a hundred pounds weight. So they took the body of Jesus and bound it in linen wrappings with the spices, as is the burial custom of the Jews."* St. John 19:38-41

The relevance of this account is *not* that Nicodemus did some good work by spending money on Jesus' burial or any other human action. This was certainly admirable, but it was not the respectful deed of giving burial ointments that saved him, but his faith in Jesus!

One last thing! Jesus testified to Nicodemus about a "Kingdom." Historically, at this time the Jews were waiting for deliverance from the oppressive government they lived under at the time and they needed a deliverer. Perhaps Nicodemus was hoping he'd found the man to lead a rebellion that unforgettable night when he made his visit. But this is not the *Kingdom* Jesus spoke about.

When I interviewed some Roman Catholic parishioners as they exited their church in one city, the overwhelming answer to a question, *"Where is the Kingdom of Heaven located?"* The majority answered that it was *"up in the sky."* I would imagine that most people think of the *Kingdom of God* is a place in the sky too! And coupled with the idea that it was *above*, those I interviewed said that you could only reach it by being good and obeying the Church till you die.

The good news is that the Kingdom begins with the presence of God in one's life. One *Other Italian* told me, *"When we enter the Kingdom, we can see God's purpose and direction for our life. Jesus becomes the Lord of our lives, and we begin to see things as we've never seen them before. The Bible calls this, "Wisdom."* It's what we need to *live our lives to the fullest; with His will and purpose in mind."* This is what happened in the life of Nicodemus and *The Other Italians!*

Chapter Two:
A Bible-Based Faith

It is not the purpose of this book to "authenticate" the Bible! A library of books has already been written that historically verify the authenticity, accuracy, and divine inspiration of the scriptures. (I might recommend a the book, "How Did We Get The Bible," written by Tracey Macon Sumner. This very readable book shows how the 66 books of the Bible were chosen to be the complete canon of scriptures accepted by both Roman Catholics and The Other Italians as the complete Bible). While there are some who believe other books are part of the canon of scriptures, these have not been authenticated.

The Other Italians do not question the legitimacy or divine inspiration of the scriptures, nor will they argue that they understand every word written therein. To begin with, Roman Catholics are taught the Church is at parity (having the same authority) with the Holy Scriptures.

These Other Italians believe in the inerrancy of the Bible. That is, it contains no errors, no discrepancies, and no conflicts. It was a most interesting exercise for me as I studied and acquired background information for this particular chapter, that I found it to be a deep root of theological conflict between the two groups, and an irreconcilable difference!

During my interviews when I questioned people about the "accuracy" of the Bible, the majority held that it contains many errors, including conflicting information with many scientific findings. For nearly one hundred years Hollywood and news media "translations" have cultivated a generation of people to rely on their very "creative" interpretation of the events in the Bible —often misquoting a verse or two. (One person I interviewed swore that Ben Hur was a man in the Bible). However, not one person I interviewed could identify a book, chapter or verse to back up their claims of error. More importantly, most were also totally unaware of important events, including those surrounding the birth, life and death of Jesus, that were actually foretold hundreds and hundreds of years before their occurrence. Scriptures regarding this phenomena are indeed profound, and worthy of a quick view!

An examination of the Old and New Testaments verifies that Jesus fulfilled over three hundred prophetic events. In 8 BC the Prophet Isaiah foretold the following event about the birth of Jesus of Nazareth.

"Therefore the Lord Himself will give you a sign: Behold, a virgin will be with child and bear a son, and she will call His name Immanuel" - (Meaning - God with us) (Isaiah 7:14)

Through the years the archaeological accuracy of the Bible has also been challenged. Incredible as it may sound, especially since the media does its best to keep a conflict ever before the public's eye, during the past fifty years more and more studies show the exactness of Biblical geography and topography.

World recognized archaeologist, Dr. Nelson Glueck confirms: "No archeological discovery has ever controverted a Biblical reference. Scores of archeological findings have been made which confirm in clear outline or in exact detail historical statements in the Bible. And, by the same token, proper evaluation of Biblical descriptions has often led to amazing discoveries."

The field of science has often been used to challenge the accuracy of the Bible, but a close examination of the scriptures finds little evidence that there is any conflict. For instance, history shows that it was not the Bible that refuted the shape of the earth but religious leaders of the time. The stigma of "religion" making the error has lasted for thousands of years. Here are a few examples of the Bible's accuracy as it relates to the "discoveries" of science. With The Other Italians, the issue is not whether the Bible can be verified scientifically but whether the scriptures confirm the findings of science:

- Shape of the earth is round (Isaiah 40:22)
- Almost infinite extent of the sidereal universe (Isaiah 55:9)
- Law of conservation of mass and energy (II Peter 3:7)
- Hydrologic cycle (Ecclesiastes 1:7)
- Innumerable stars (Jeremiah 33:22)
- Law of increasing entropy (Psalm 102:25-27)
- Paramount importance of blood in life processes (Lev17:11)
- Atmospheric circulation (Ecclesiastes 1:6)
- Gravitational field (Job 26:7)

These are just a few examples! Again, it is not the intent of this author to verify or test the scriptures, but to show the reliance The Other Italians have in them! One of the things this group has learned is that the Bible can be relied on to help and direct their lives. They say daily reading gives continuous insight into the issues of life. Yet, ask the man on the street if the Bible is difficult to understand, and you can expect an answer in the affirmative.

The New American Standard Bible (Approved for Roman Catholic reading), written in the early English vernacular, poses another roadblock for some readers. One interviewee shared - "Words like, "thus" and "thou," "shalt" and "saith," in many translations are considered archaic. Yet, these same individuals have no objection with the stories of Willie Shakespeare, who wrote in the same dialect."

When questioned, The Other Italians told me that the scriptures are relatively easy to understand. Early on, many Italian immigrants with limited education were introduced to the Biblical plan of salvation, and fervently began to read and follow the scriptures. For the new Italian immigrant, many of whose passports classified them as "peasants," the Bible, written in the Italian language, was considered to be an easy reader. Later on they told their children and grandchildren about the impact the scriptures had on their lives, and the decision they had made that fateful day when they turned their life over to their Lord Jesus.

Today, generation's later, entire family "lines" adhere to the Biblical plan of salvation through the exercise of their personal faith. They read the Bible, studied it, and with the illumination of the Holy Spirit (Jesus predicted this), understood and accepted its message of salvation through faith alone in Jesus; thus rejecting any doctrine that was contrary to the scriptures. The message to Nicodemus was simple; a man or woman no matter how intelligent they may be cannot understand the scriptures unless the Holy Spirit illumines their heart.

According to The Other Italians, when an individual recognizes their spiritual state, and the provision of Jesus to forgive them, it is the beginning of a "life in Christ." A person must understand who Jesus is! Obviously, the Disciples came to that conviction.

The Bible records an important day in St. Peter's life when he declared, by faith, the deity of Jesus of Nazareth. Peter was presented with a question…the question all people must answer to see and enter the Kingdom of God. Permit me to phrase the question in our present day language: "Hey, Pete, I've been with you quite a while now…the other people around are guessing who I am…but who do you think I am?" Here's his answer found in St. Matthew 16:16, "Thou art the Christ, the Son of the Living God!" Jesus responds, "Peter, man did not illumine this to you…but the Spirit of My Father in heaven!" Peter's declaration is the key to understanding the new life in Christ Jesus! It is the "key" to the kingdom for the individual.

Further along in the scriptures, after the resurrection, Jesus greets two men who were walking on a road to the City of Emmaus. They didn't know who he was when they first engaged him in conversation. Here's the record in the scripture: "He explained to them the things concerning Himself in all the Scriptures." Then He sat down with them and something extraordinary happened as Jesus continued to expound the Scriptures to them; "Then their eyes were opened and they recognized Him;" (Luke 24:27, 31). The

Other Italians confirm that they too had their eyes opened when they recognized who Jesus is when they read the scriptures for themselves! The scriptures confirm the deity of Jesus!

St. John 16:13 shares the words of Jesus to His Disciples during His last days on earth while ministering to them: "But when He, the Spirit of truth, comes, He will guide you into all the truth; for He will not speak on His own initiative, but whatever He hears, He will speak; and He will disclose to you what is to come."

Yes, those turn-of-the-century Italian immigrants began to rely on the Holy Spirit within them, rather than the dogma of the Church. This still holds today with millions upon millions of Other Italians who have also come to a point where they totally rely on the Holy Spirit to inspire and guide them as they read the scriptures.

When St. Peter declared Jesus was the Son of God, it was the Holy Spirit that confirmed that within him. Peter clarified the role of God's Holy Spirit in his second letter, and shows the means by which the Bible was given to mankind: "But know this first of all, that no prophecy of Scripture is a matter of one's own interpretation, for no prophecy was ever made by an act of human will, but men moved by the Holy Spirit spoke from God." (2 Peter 1:20)

To be concise, these scripture confirm that nothing written in the Bible represents the writer's own understanding of things! What this verse does not say is that the average man or woman cannot read and apply the scriptures to their everyday living! It does say with the "illumination" of the Holy Spirit in one's life, the scriptures come alive and are meaningful!

The Other Italians have come to a point where they read, believe and rely on the Holy Scriptures to guide their life. Reading the Bible becomes something that is part of their existence as a Christian, and it is the classroom where they study. They accept the Bible as the inspired Word of God, and as a result, trust Him to be in their lives on a daily basis. The Other Italians will tell you the end result is a strengthening of their "personal relationship" with Jesus. The Holy Spirit is the one who must illumines the Scripture in a person's heart and mind. I remember the words of one interviewee who said, "Hey, don't believe me…read the Bible, He's in there for the reading!"

THE HOLY BIBLE AND CHURCH TRADITION

Tradition plays a significant role in the life of a Roman Catholic. Participating in the sacramental rituals of the Church is a mandatory obligation, although only a few have a scriptural basis. Members are taught that the Church holds equal authority with the Bible and members must accept the connection between tradition, ritual and scripture. In the Catechism of the Church, paragraph 97 it reads: "Sacred Tradition and Sacred Scripture make up a single sacred deposit of the Word of God." Paragraph 82 reads: "Both Scripture and Tradition must be accepted and honored with equal sentiments of devotion and reverence."

The Other Italians understand that traditions change but the Bible is invariable. In St. Paul's letter to the Church in Colossae, he cautioned the congregation with these words: "See to it that no one takes you captive through philosophy and empty deception, according to the tradition of men, according to the elementary principles of the world, rather than according to Christ." (Colossians 2:8) The Word of God is changeless! St. Matthew's gospel records the words of Jesus "Heaven and earth will pass away, but My words will not pass away." (Matthew 24:35)

"Sacred traditions" (as identified by the Church) are created by humans, and over the years are adopted and given great importance in Church worship. In time some of these are incorporated into the dictum or dictates of the Church, and some are discarded.

Interestingly, some of these have been discovered to be unfounded. As a result, they have been eliminated from the Canon of Laws. The authority to change the Canon laws governing the Church rests in the Office of the Pope, but there are also other things the Roman Catholic Church believes he has the authority to do. "The Pope has the power to change times, to abrogate laws, and to dispense with all things, even the precepts of Christ." "The Pope has the authority and often exercised it, to dispense with the command of Christ." -Decretal, de Tranlatic Episcop. Cap. (The Pope can modify divine law.) Ferraris' Ecclesiastical Dictionary.

The Other Italians cannot accept this boundless authority of the Pope and ask; does he have the authority to question, change or alter the commandments of Jesus? They can no longer accept the idea that a mortal man can dispense with all things…including the laws of Christ Jesus. Human laws and traditions cannot subjugate the Bible. An example of the "changing beliefs," of the Church is seen in the theology of LIMBO. For centuries Roman Catholics were taught this is where babies go when they die if the Church has not baptized them. The Other Italians know there is no Biblical basis for this belief.

The International Theological Commission (Roman Catholic appointees). Here are their findings on the subject of LIMBO: "It is clear that the traditional teaching on this topic has concentrated on the theory of limbo, understood as a state which includes the souls of infants who die subject to original sin and without baptism, and who, therefore, neither merit the beatific vision, nor yet are subjected to any punishment, because they are not guilty of any personal sin. This theory, elaborated by theologians beginning in the Middle Ages, never entered into the dogmatic definitions of the Magisterium, even if that same Magisterium did at times mention the theory in its ordinary teaching up until the Second Vatican Council. It remains therefore a possible theological hypothesis. However, in the Catechism of the Catholic Church (1992), the theory of limbo is not mentioned. Rather, the Catechism teaches that infants who die without baptism are entrusted by the Church to the mercy of God, as is shown in the specific funeral rite for such children. The principle that God desires the salvation of all people gives rise to the hope that there is a path to salvation for infants who die without baptism (cf. CCC, 1261), and therefore also to the theological desire to find a coherent and logical connection between the diverse affirmations of the Catholic faith: the universal salvific will of God; the unicity of the mediation of Christ; the necessity of baptism for salvation; the universal action of grace in relation to the sacraments; the link between original sin and the deprivation of the beatific vision; the creation of man "in Christ."

The conclusion of this study is that there are theological and liturgical reasons to hope that infants who die without baptism may be saved and brought into eternal happiness, even if there is not an explicit teaching on this question found in Revelation. However, none of the considerations proposed in this text to motivate a new approach to the question may be used to negate the necessity of baptism, nor to delay the conferral of the sacrament. Rather, there are reasons to hope that God will save these infants precisely because it was not possible to do for them that what would have been most desirable to baptize them in the faith of the Church and incorporate them visibly into the Body of Christ."

Those Roman Catholics, with whom I shared the above text, were nothing less than angry. They had been taught that LIMBO was a real place for un-baptized babies. Without LIMBO they had no idea where some of the children in their family now rested, having not been baptized before passing. It has only been in recent days that the Church has abandoned their ideas about LIMBO.

Few of my respondents knew the teaching of "Limbo" had been eliminated!

Reuter News Service (April 2007) reported – "The Roman Catholic Church has effectively buried the concept of limbo, the place where centuries of tradition and teaching held that babies who die without baptism went. In a long-awaited document, the Church's International Theological Commission said limbo reflected an 'unduly restrictive view of salvation'. The 41-page document was published on Friday by Origins, the documentary service of the U.S.-based Catholic News Service, which is part of the U.S. Conference of Catholic Bishop. Pope Benedict, himself a top theologian who before his election in 2005 expressed doubts about limbo, authorized the publication of the document, called "The Hope of Salvation for Infants Who Die Without Being Baptized." The verdict that limbo could now rest in peace had been expected for years. The document was seen as most likely the final word since limbo was never part of Church doctrine, even though it was taught to Catholics well into the 20th century."

The Church teaches that baptism removes original sin which stains all souls since the fall from grace in the Garden of Eden. Limbo, which comes from the Latin word meaning "border" or "edge,", was considered by medieval theologians to be a state or place reserved for the un-baptized dead, including good people who lived before the coming of Christ. People find it increasingly difficult to accept that God is just and merciful if he excludes infants, who have no personal sins, from eternal happiness, whether they are Christian or non-Christian; the number of non-baptised infants has grown considerably, and therefore the reflection on the possibility of salvation for these infants has become urgent."

The commission's conclusions had been widely expected. In writings before his election as Pope in 2005, the then Cardinal Joseph Ratzinger made it clear he believed the concept of limbo should be abandoned because it was "only a theological hypothesis" and "never a defined truth of faith." In the Divine Comedy, Dante placed virtuous pagans and great classical philosophers, including Plato and Socrates, in limbo. The Catholic Church's official catechism, issued in 1992 after decades of work, dropped the mention of limbo." (These days, under such circumstances, one might conclude that that "Divine Comedy" was neither divine nor comedic!)

The Other Italians I interviewed regarding this issue, site such church "hypothetical and theoretical ideas" as inconsistent with the overall text of salvation for the individual as presented in the Bible. They refuse to accept a "possible theoretical hypothesis" as a tenet of their faith.

The Apostle Paul wrote a couple of letters to a young man named Timothy about his assurance of God's promise to save and keep him: "for I know whom I have believed, and am convinced that he is able to guard what I have entrusted to Him until that day!" (2 Timothy 1:12)

In a letter to the Church in Rome, Paul wrote: "For I am convinced that neither death, nor life, nor angels, nor principalities, nor things present, nor things to come, nor powers, nor height, nor depth, nor any other created thing, will be able to separate us from the love of God, which is in Christ Jesus our Lord." (Romans 8: 38-39)

The "open-ended" theory of an impending decision on God's part to save a child was already discarded by The Other Italians over a century ago. There is no Biblical foundation for this ancient belief! As for the eternal destiny of un-baptized children, they adhere to the personal accountability of the individual in such matters, and this occurs when any individual has reached an age of maturity and understanding of their spiritual condition. Obviously, the age of accountability is different for each child.

SCRIPTURE AND RITUAL

As already stated, The Other Italians place their confidence and trust in the Bible; they say it is their guidebook for daily living. They are actively and continually engaged in learning more about the provisions God has for them, and they accept the Bible as their only source. They hold that "Apostolic tradition" or the Church's magisterium (authority) is not needed to interpret or decode what the scriptures say or mean; truth is found in the Bible, and any peripheral authority, directives, hypothetical theories or oral traditions with speculative interpretations are rejected.

Through the years, the best attempt of theologians to interpret the scriptures has sometimes been flawed, but the basic truths are evident. The Other Italians contend that too often theological ideas are based on isolated scriptures or erroneous or flawed interpretations. (These will be considered in the following chapters).

The Roman Catholic Church does not recognize the Bible as a "stand alone source" or independent foundation of spiritual authority. The Bible, plus apostolic tradition, and the authority of the Church is what lies at the underpinning of Roman Catholic faith. Only the Church has the authority to interpret the Holy Scriptures.

The Other Italians reject the idea of "peripheral authority," and have found the power of the scriptures alone to speak to them. They say if we want to be sure of interpreting the Bible correctly, we must permit the Holy Spirit to help and preserve us from misinterpreting or misunderstanding. They will tell you that the Author of the scriptures is surely able to reveal them. He is able to confirm what His Word says. A person who does not have the Holy Spirit within will find many things about the Scriptures to be puzzling. The Apostle Paul sheds light on this when he wrote: "But a natural man does not accept the things of the Spirit of God, for they are foolishness to him; and he cannot understand them, because they are spiritually appraised." (1 Corinthians 2:14)

Here's that scripture as written in the Living Bible version: "But the man who isn't a Christian can't understand and can't accept these thoughts from God, which the Holy Spirit teaches us. They sound foolish to him because only those who have the Holy Spirit within them can understand what the Holy Spirit means. Others just can't take it in."

But for those who are born again Paul writes: "Now we have received, not the spirit of the world, but the Spirit who is from God, so that we may know the things freely given to us by God," (1 Cor. 2:12).

The individual who has experienced a spiritual "new birth" becomes spiritually literate!

In the Second Vatican Council's document on divine revelation we see the mandate of the Church as it relates to the Bible: "Hence there exists a close connection and communication between sacred tradition and sacred Scripture. For both of them, flowing from the same divine wellspring, in a certain way merge into a unity and tend toward the same end. For sacred Scripture is the word of God inasmuch as it is consigned to writing, under the inspiration of the divine Spirit. To the successors of the apostles, sacred tradition hands on in its full purity God's word, which was entrusted to the apostles by Christ the Lord and the Holy Spirit. Thus, by the light of the Spirit of truth, these successors can in their preaching preserve this word of God faithfully, explain it, and make it more widely known. Consequently it is not from sacred Scripture alone that the Church draws her certainty about everything which has been revealed. Therefore both sacred Tradition and sacred Scripture are to be accepted and venerated with the same devotion and reverence."

Much of what is taught in the Roman Catholic Church is confessed as "Institutional Tradition." To The Other Italians such rituals and practices have no foundation in the Bible and are rejected. It is no secret that The Roman Catholic Church operates under its own authority. Again, The Other Italians deny this premise and adhere to what is known as SOLA SCRIPTURA…or the scriptures alone. To add any idea, theory or tenet to the Bible is to concede that it is not complete and extra revelation is needed. Yet, consider these scriptures in the light of this, another, irreconcilable difference:

"You shall not add to the word which I am commanding you, nor take away from it, that you may keep the commandments of the Lord your God which I command you." (Deuteronomy 4:2)

"Whatever I command you, you shall be careful to do; you shall not add to nor take away from it." (Deuteronomy 12:32)

"Every word of God is tested; He is a shield to those who take refuge in Him. Do not add to His words or He will reprove you, and you will be proved a liar." (Proverbs 30:5-6)

"and if anyone takes away from the words of the book of this prophecy, God will take away his part from the tree of life and from the holy city, which are written in this book." (Revelation 22:19)

In another letter to young Timothy, the Apostle Paul wrote about the purpose of the scriptures: "All Scripture is inspired by God and profitable for teaching, for reproof, for correction, for training in righteousness; so that the man of God may be adequate, equipped for every good work." (2 Timothy 3:16-17)

The Bible never mentions any other source for interpretation nor does it specifically say, allude, recommend, offer or in any way decree one needs something or someone other than the presence of the Holy Spirit to understand the scriptures. One of The Other Italians I interviewed said: "One gets to know God by reading His blueprint, and allowing His spirit from within to reveal the meaning and application of the scriptures!"

Saint John wrote in his Gospel a summation of the reasons why he told the story of Jesus: "Therefore many other signs Jesus also performed in the presence of the disciples, which are not written in this book; but these have been written so that you may believe that Jesus is the Christ, the Son of God; and that believing you may have life in His name." (John 20:30-31)

These Other Italians believe that everything we need to know about Jesus Christ is in the scriptures that reveal Him!

The Other Italians accept only the original, and as the expression goes, accept no substitutes, additions or on-going re-interpretations. They believe the Bible stands alone, and allow the Holy Spirit within them to "reveal" the meaning and purpose of the scriptures.

In Jesus' explanation to Nicodemus about being born again, He speaks of the Spirit of God in terms of breathing on and within the individual. This is indeed a mystery to some, while it is reality to others. They hold to the promise of the Lord, who said: But when He, the Spirit of truth, comes, He will guide you into all the truth; for He will not speak on His own initiative, but whatever He hears, He will speak; and He will disclose to you what is to come. He will glorify Me, for He will take of Mine and will disclose it to you. All things that the Father has are Mine; therefore I said that He takes of Mine and will disclose it to you." (St. John 16:13-15):

In a bold statement, a minister, and theologian within this Italian community told me the following: "The scholar and sophisticate, without the Spirit of Christ at work within him or her; who knows Greek and Hebrew, and understands clearly the words on the page, will never find the message of God in the scriptures! They can become experts in the letter of the Word, and be without the Spirit of Jesus!"

The Bible gives no evidence that an organization has the authority or "special revelation or insight" to enlighten the scriptures for an individual. The Bible record is that Jesus is the central figure of the Church…not a man or a woman!

Events that have made the scriptures easier to understand include the knowledge scholars have gained during the past one hundred years about the languages of the original texts. The scriptures were written and translated in Hebrew, Arabic, Greek and Latin; today we have a more precise knowledge of context (background), word origin and meaning (Morphology), sentence structure (configuration or syntax), and semantics (symbolic language). Modern literal interpretations of the Bible are readily available and support the message that the scriptures stand alone ("Sola Scriptura").

Reading the scriptures and understanding them are two distinct things! Nicodemus had read the scriptures but never saw the real message of redemption. In contrast to the view of Sola Scriptura is the idea that the Pope is infallible, has the power to speak for God, and interpret the scriptures. In fact, the Canon of the Church declares the Pope cannot be overruled!

The Other Italians find no Biblical premise, (explicit or inferential) for Papal authority, and their research sites examples of Papal conflict in leadership. The authority to discern the scriptures on behalf of a billion members of the Church, hinges on Papal succession. Uninterrupted papal succession has been the foundation of the office! But as a matter of fact, at four times in Roman Catholic history there were two Popes competing for control of the Church. The question to be answered is this? Which one was infallible? Which one was the Vicar of God? Under such circumstances, which Pope would have the first and final say on interpreting the scriptures?

Nowhere in the Bible is anyone appointed to speak on behalf of God other than Jesus. Here is His declaration of authority as recorded in the scripture with the words: "I and my Father are one!" (St. John 1:30) At no time did Jesus ever share His divine authority or appoint anyone to speak for the scriptures. St. Matthew chronicles the same message: "And Jesus came up and spoke to them, saying, "All authority has been given to Me in heaven and on earth! (St. Matthew 28:18)

Has God shared His divine authority with anyone other than His son? The Bible does not bear record of any divine transmission of power to any mortal. Interestingly, my own research showed that before 1059 AD, Popes were actually chosen by their predecessors or secular rulers, thus circumventing the line of succession. The historic record of papal succession found in book, THE BLOODY THEATER or MARTYRS MIRROR OF THE DEFENSELESS CHRISTIANS (Thieleman J. Van Braght – John F. Sohm, Translator Date of Publication 1660), documents periods where there were two, three and four Popes, simultaneously sitting as the head of the Church in several countries in Europe at the same time.

Again, The Other Italians believe the Holy Spirit is the one that illumines the scriptures. They also believe the Holy Spirit, dwelling within the individual, confirms them. St. John assured his readers: "But the Helper, the Holy Spirit, whom the Father will send in My name, He will teach you all things," (John 14:26)

"But when He, the Spirit of truth, comes, He will guide you into all the truth; for He will not speak on His own initiative, but whatever He hears, He will speak; and He will disclose to you what is to come." (John 16:13)

The continuing theme throughout the scriptures is that only the Holy Spirit, dwelling within the individual, can illumine the truths contained therein. That indwelling comes with the new birth. St. Paul declared the following in a letter to the Corinthians: "Now we have received, not the spirit of the world, but the Spirit who is from God, so that we may know the things freely given to us by God, which things we also speak, not in words taught by human wisdom, but in those taught by the Spirit, combining spiritual thoughts with spiritual words." (Corinthians 2:12-13)

Consider the words of St. Peter and the life The Other Italians now claim. "For you have been born again not of seed which is perishable but imperishable, that is, through the living and enduring word of God. For, all flesh is like grass, and all its glory like the flower of grass. The grass withers, and the flower falls off, But the word of the Lord endures forever." 1 Peter 1: 23-25)

Here's that scripture passage from the Living Bible: "For you have a new life. It was not passed on to you from your parents, for the life they gave you will fade away. This new one will last forever, for it comes from Christ, God's ever-living Message to men. Yes, our natural lives will fade as grass does when it becomes all brown and dry. All our greatness is like a flower that droops and falls; but the Word of the Lord will last forever. And his message is the Good News that was preached to you!"

The Other Italians have the assurance of salvation, eternity in heaven, and while on earth, the comfort of the Holy Spirit that Jesus promised would lead them into all truth! The Holy Bible is the sole basis for what they believe.

Chapter Three:
Fundamental Questions

The primary differences between The Other Italians and Roman Catholic Italians center on two questions:

QUESTION NUMBER ONE

What is the New Testament Church?

The Other Italians believe the Church of Jesus is essentially invisible and spiritual; that it's made up of all believers who have experienced the New Birth by the power of the Holy Spirit, and that no earthly organization can corporately assume to be "THE" Church or claim to control the destiny of any individual.

Roman Catholics hold that the New Testament Church, which emanated from the time of Christ's ministry, is a physical-spiritual organization on earth and is headed by a leader. Its leader is called, "Pope!" While they believe the Church is a spiritual reality, they hold that the Church of Rome is the only "true" church on earth because of its continuous structural succession over the centuries.

Documented history does not support this premise!

As students of the Bible, The Other Italians reference the original Greek and Hebrew translations and understand that the word, "church," in the

New Testament is translated "ecclesia," and never refers to any earthly organization or entity. "Ecclesia" simply means "a gathering of people."

The Other Italians never reference the "New Testament Church" in these terms: as a physical building, denomination, cult or organization - whether local, regional or international. These individuals consider themselves to be part of a group of "believers," and view the church as those who have be regenerated by the power of the Holy Spirit." The word, "church" certainly can be used for an assembly of believers, as long as it is understood that we are talking about PEOPLE, and not an organization or institution. The early church was actually made up of small groups or cells.

QUESTION NUMBER TWO
What is the means of God's grace?

Roman Catholics believe that God's saving grace comes to the individual through the sacraments. In one sacrament, the MASS, Christ is received into the physical body, through the mouth by a consecrated wafer of bread (referred to as, "The Host," once it is transformed into the actual body of Jesus) administered by a duly ordained priest. The priest, who officiates this transformation and administers the same, must be linked to a human succession originating with the Apostle Peter, and descending to the present day for him to perform the ceremony. Thus the Church member must regularly partake in the Church's sacraments to receive pardon for their sins. It is an on-going process. There is no finality in the Mass, which The Other Italians believe is a conflict with the scriptural teaching that Christ died once and for all.

The Other Italians believe that God's saving grace comes by simple faith alone. No personal action or work is necessary to achieve forgiveness, as God's grace is not manifested through the mandates or ceremonies of any institution; they believe God's grace is free and abundant to everyone. After they have been reconciled to God, they believe one can "grow in faith" by reading the scriptures and hearing the preaching of the Gospel. St. Paul wrote:

"And when I came to you, brethren, I did not come with superiority of speech or of wisdom, proclaiming to you the testimony of God." Here's the same verse in the Living Bible translation: "When I first came to you, dear brothers and sisters I didn't use lofty words and impressive wisdom to tell you God's secret plans." 1 Corinthians 2:1

The Other Italians recognize the importance of "hearing" (internalizing) the Word of God in their own devotion, and from those who are called to preach and teach. The Bible puts it this way as written by St. Paul to the church in Rome "Faith cometh by hearing and hearing by the Word of God." (Romans, chapter 10:17)

They accept the grace of God to forgive them, as a free gift, paid for when Jesus went to the cross and died ONCE and for all for the forgiveness of sins. (I placed an emphasis on the word once as they believe Jesus accomplished the work of grace on the cross in those moments when He surrendered His life for the sin of all mankind). Their understanding of the scriptures is that there is nothing they can do to earn it in any way and understand it is there's for the asking.

Again, let's look at the Apostle Paul's letter to the believers in Rome. Romans, Chapter 10 verses 9-13. The Other Italians hold to this promise of the scriptures that says: "that if you confess with your mouth Jesus as Lord, and believe in your heart that God raised Him from the dead, you will be saved; for with the heart a person believes, resulting in righteousness, and with the mouth he confesses, resulting in salvation. For the Scripture says, "Whoever believes in Him will not be disappointed." For there is no distinction between Jew and Greek; for the same Lord is Lord of all, abounding in riches for all who call on Him; for "Whoever will call on the name of the Lord will be saved." The Other Italians believe this and have accepted it as the only way to salvation.

Note: Nowhere in the Bible is there mention of a church organization or institution that can save us - or an absolute church leader to govern the physical or invisible church - or a system of repentance whereby the individual must do something to achieve salvation other than by exercising faith.

Equally important is that there is no scripture that gives anyone, at anytime, permanent, transient or temporary authorization, whereby they can go directly to God on another person's behalf, and ask for forgiveness for his or her sins. The Other Italians believe only Jesus can do that for you.

The Other Italians believe God's forgiving and saving grace is free...because that is the reason why Jesus went to the Cross - died and came forth from the grave. God's provision for all of mankind was the death of his Son - a complete, and final ONE TIME sacrifice. The idea that any earthly institution can absolve sin remains an irreconcilable difference!

The question repeats itself and has for over two thousand years. If there was or is any way to achieve salvation, why did Jesus have to go to the cross and die?

In summary: The Other Italians believe the church on earth is invisible and includes every person of any age, race, and culture whose sins are forgiven through the death and resurrection of Jesus Christ, and who have been regenerated by the power of the Holy Spirit.

Chapter Four:
What is The Nature of Sin?

The Other Italians hold to the scriptures in answering questions relating to mankind's spiritual condition. Simply stated, sin separates the creation from the creator. Central to the theme of "sin" is the scriptural declaration! "For all have sinned and fall short of the glory of God." (Romans 3:23)

The Biblical message states: Jesus died for the sins of the whole world. WHY? The Other Italians understand that everyone who has ever lived, is living or will live is a sinner in the sight of God! Revealing, is the fact that humans have a shown a profound understanding of this as historical documents, art forms and traditions yield to the premise of man's depravity.

If you visit the Sistine Chapel and view some of the Frescos, you'll see that the subject is "sin." In one example, there is a depiction of Adam and Eve being cast out of the Garden of Eden because they sinned by disobeying God. They did something He forbade (Eating of the Tree of Knowledge of Good and Evil), and the "casting out" meant separation. Art forms for thousands of years have portrayed good and evil. The expression that there is "a little bit of good and bad in everyone," identifies the inclination of humankind to identify both sides of the behavioral coin.

The scriptures are not shallow in confirming the "root" of sin, and it's more than a little enlightening! "The one who practices sin is of the devil;

for the devil has sinned from the beginning. The Son of God appeared for this purpose, to destroy the works of the devil." (1 John 3:8). This scripture comes as a rude awakening to those who find intellectual reasoning and sanctuary in the ideas behind the "Yin and Yang."

The Other Italians rely on the scriptures that say Jesus did not come to bond or blend in with the devil. No, He came to annihilate him, and did that when He came forth from the grave thereby eliminating the final hold Satan had on humans: DEATH!

During the last century, the issue of sin has become a topic of songs, novels, poems, movie themes and other media expressions. A popular rock n' roll song of the mid-twentieth century promised - "I'll never, never, ever tell another white lie!" And an even older generation will remember the song made famous by a group called the Ink Spots, "It's a sin to tell a lie," while a younger set heard the lyrics from a song titled, "Lying Eyes." A famous perfume was even named, "MY SIN." In these settings, and others, sin becomes a frivolous idea to be tolerated, understood, accepted and even enjoyed as a normal and acceptable form of human behavior - although still (for the time being) uncharacteristic, in the truest sense, of society's moral and religious teaching. We live in a time when people are titillated with the idea of doing wrong, and getting away with it! With the present generation, "sin" has been reduced to "being bad," and by today's thinking, human behavior that doesn't harm others can't be all that bad! While it may not be offensive to others, The Other Italians are aware that it is offensive to God! The issue is not what we think of sin but what God thinks about it and how He deals with it.

Once they began to read the Bible, The Other Italians came to know the meaning and consequences of sin. Based on their reading and understanding of the scriptures, they will tell you, like Nicodemus of old, at one time their sin separated them from God too.

They were spiritually blinded by it.

The Bible clearly states that God cannot be in the presence of sin. So someone had to remove that which blocked mankind's relationship with God; and that it is SIN. This is the reason why Jesus came, died and rose from the dead. Jesus took the sin of every individual on Himself. Now, get this picture! Jesus, the Son of God, is hanging on a cross, with the sins of everyone who has ever lived, was living and who will ever live; He has all of their sin on Himself. The consequence? God could not look at His own Son while hanging on the cross!

Ever wonder why that at the site of the crucifixion Jesus cried out, "My God, My God, Why hast thou forsaken me!" Why would God dissert His only begotten Son? The reason is profound and reveals His character! God is Holy and He cannot be in the presence of sin. The Other Italians understand the scriptures, which proclaim that Jesus not only took our sins to the cross, but also became sin for us! This truth is found in a letter the Apostle Paul wrote to the Church in Corinth: "He made Him who knew no sin to be sin on our behalf, so that we might become the righteousness of God in Him." (2 Corinthians 5:21)

Wow, that's heavy…but so are the consequences of sin! This message is sobering! Sin is the reason why mankind cannot fellowship with their heavenly Father. This was presented in Chapter One of this book when Nicodemus met Jesus. St. Paul reminded the Corinthians about Jesus' role in man's redemption, and that God made no exceptions in His appraisal of mankind: "For all have sinned and come short of the glory of God."(Romans 3:23)

Jesus took upon himself the sins of the whole world! The Other Italians will tell you that the first thing they recognized in their quest to have a relationship with God is that they were sinners. They came to understand the sin-nature with which they came into the world; that they were destined to sin, and that since the beginning of time, with the exception of Jesus, everyone has sinned. Roman Catholics believe this too and that's why they baptize infants as soon as possible and adults celebrate the Mass to keep renewing God's grace on their life! We don't like to think of ourselves as sinners, but the Bible informs us of our true nature and our potential behavior. Sin is inescapable, no matter how hard we try to avoid it in our lives.

The Bible reference about this is found throughout the New Testament. The book, written by the Apostle Paul to the Romans spells out in a few words in Chapter 5: 12: "Therefore, just as through one man sin entered into the world, and death (spiritual death) through sin, and so death (spiritual death) spread to all men, because all sinned."

It would be nice to make an exemption for our fathers, mothers and even the most "religious" person we know. But the scriptures are all inclusive; EVERYONE HAS SINNED, and no individual or institution can assert that someone is without sin, take it away, wipe it out, absolve or pardon it. The question that shows the conflict between what The Other Italians believe and the Roman Catholic Church is this! How can an individual, group or an institution who have sinned, declare that someone is sinless? No one has that authority other than Jesus!

Nowhere in the Bible is there an exception to this scripture, "All have sinned." The Other Italians do not recognize any individual as ever having lived without sin…even if the Roman Catholic Church declares that someone is sinless. There are no exclusions, as the Holy Bible remains the only source The Other Italians embrace. This matter stands as an irreconcilable difference!

BUT AREN'T THERE DIFFERENT KINDS OF SIN?

If we take a moment to decide the gravity of certain sinful behaviors we have to conclude that there are big sins, little sins, and there are a whole lot in between. We can also rank sins by their impact on the individual who sins, and the impact on others. In some cases we can even "justify" our wrong doing with some kind of intellectual rationale. But no matter how we justify our sinful behavior we cannot embrace a God who is Holy in our sinful state.

As stated, the idea of sin or sinning has been chronicled in music, literature, and many other art forms, and is something we hear about every day of our lives courtesy of the media. Good and evil are the central themes in the story of human behavior. No culture has ever escaped sin's impact, and the consequence it has on individuals, and whole civilizations is part of our recorded history.

The Biblical message is clear, sin separates us from God. Whether or not we judge it in ourselves first, and then in others, God is judging it! If we want God in our lives, the sin has to go! It's a choice everyone has to make. It's the choice The Other Italians have made!

Should we be held accountable to innumerate our sins before God, we'd be confessing a million sins of the past, a whole lot in the present and would have to stand ready to do some explaining for our future faults too. There is however one word that encompasses all of our unrighteousness before God. The word is "sinner!"

But how about the "little white lie?" Does that really count? And what of the three year old who looks at his parents with a straight face and declares, "I didn't hit Benny," or "I didn't eat the candy on the table!" These are lies understandable from only one viewpoint. We are born with a nature that will inevitably cause us to sin.

Catholic Priest and scholar, Saint Augustine of Hippo (354–430) explained this way: "Man inherits a tendency to sin which always, sooner or later and to some extent makes itself manifest!"

This present generation has made light of sin demonstrated by the comedian who told his audiences, "The devil made me do it!" Nothing could more profound than that statement. The problem is that people chuckle when they hear this comedic excuse!

If God is Holy and He formed humans…where did the sin come from? The Other Italians recognize that Satan is the father of lies. Consider the words of St. John in this matter: "You are of your father the devil, and you want to do the desires of your father. He was a murderer from the beginning, and does not stand in the truth because there is no truth in him. Whenever he speaks a lie, he speaks from his own nature, for he is a liar and the father of lies." (St. John 8:44)

Satan's sin was rebellion against God and he's in the business taking down everyone he can! The Other Italians said they had a choice to make: "Give God control of their lives or Satan?" And he's not a little red-faced man with horns in his head and a spear in his hand. The spiritual revelation comes when an individual finally sees his mentor, Satan, for who he is, and what he wants to accomplish in his or her life. Satan wants to devour mankind and he is the spirit of everything that God is not!

The devil does make us do it if we make the conscious decision to yield to him. Consider the words of St. Peter 5:8: "Be of sober spirit, be on the alert. Your adversary, the devil, prowls around like a roaring lion, seeking someone to devour."

The Other Italians recognize they contend with Satan's many devices to seduce and ultimately destroy! His agenda is to influence the mind of people. His methods are tantalizing, glamorous, disguised, and camouflaged! One who is in "spiritual darkness" cannot see him for who he is and what he does!

Consider the words of St Paul's letter to the Church in Ephesus: "For our struggle is not against flesh and blood, but against the rulers, against the powers, against the world forces of this darkness, against the spiritual forces of wickedness in the heavenly places." (Ephesians 6:12)

Now for a modern translation: "For we are not fighting against people made of flesh and blood, but against persons without bodies, the evil rulers of the unseen world, those mighty satanic beings and great evil princes of darkness who rule this world; and against huge numbers of wicked spirits in the spirit world." (Living Bible)

According to the scriptures, there is a battle going on in the heavens for the souls of men and women! Satan on one hand is the great deceiver who influences, and is in the business of destroying people. One the other hand is Jesus who outstretches one hand to humanity, while clutching the hand of God the Father. That's quite a visual and is a simple image to keep in mind. When there is no room for Satan to invade the mind and heart…the Bible says, "He flees!" Here's the Bible on it: "Submit therefore to God. Resist the devil and he will flee from you." (St. James 4:7)

The Other Italians no longer submit to a Church, but to God. They state that all the insight and reason they need to do this is found in the Bible. They are confident that Jesus is ever present on this earth, in their home, and in their heart.

There is a basic belief The Other Italians embrace: That Jesus died for the sins they committed in the past…are committing now and will commit.

That doesn't give them the "license" to sin but the assurance of God's forgiving grace in their lives.

The Other Italians do not perceive God as some great unreachable power, dressed in white, sitting on throne somewhere up in the heavens (Hollywood version). They recognize that God's presence is within them because Jesus has cleansed them from sin. It is a "done deal!" Yes, one must recognize the wrongdoing, the sins in his or her life and repent; but they have the assurance that Jesus is ever making provision for them at the feet of God the Father: "Christ Jesus is He who died, yes, rather who was raised, who is at the right hand of God, who also intercedes for us!" (Romans 8:34) If we back up a few verses to Romans 8:1 we receive quite a revelation: "Therefore there is now no condemnation for those who are in Christ Jesus."

IS JESUS THE ONLY INTERCESSOR?

Nowhere in the Bible is there any indication that any man or woman, dead or alive can make intercession to God on behalf of our sins. The Other Italians site these scriptures with reference to sin and intercession:

Isaiah 64:6: "For all of us have become like one who is unclean, And all our righteous deeds are like a filthy garment; And all of us wither like a leaf, And our iniquities, like the wind, take us away."

Proverbs 28:13: "He who conceals his transgressions will not prosper, But he who confesses and forsakes them will find compassion."

Hosea 5:15: "I will go and return to my place, till they acknowledge their offence, and seek my face: in their affliction they will seek me early."

1 John 1:7-9: "But if we walk in the Light as He Himself is in the Light, we have fellowship with one another, and the blood of Jesus His Son cleanses us from all sin. If we say that we have no sin, we are deceiving ourselves and the truth is not in us. If we confess our sins, He is faithful and righteous to forgive us our sins and to cleanse us from all unrighteousness."

- 1 Corinthians 15:57: "But thanks be to God, who gives us the victory through our Lord Jesus Christ."

- Romans 8:1: "Therefore there is now no condemnation for those who are in Christ Jesus."
- Romans 3:23: "For all have sinned and fall short of the Glory of God!"

The Other Italians have discovered for themselves the remedy for sin! It's found in St. John's gospel 1:12: "But as many as received Him, to them He gave the right to become children of God, even to those who believe in His name."

They understand the scriptures that testify to the following:
- God is holy and cannot be in the presence of sin
- Sin separates us from god
- Everyone who has ever lived has sinned
- Satan is the father of sin
- Sin destroys the individual
- Sin is the reason why Jesus had to die
- Sin is cleansed by the blood of Jesus
- Jesus now presents us faultless before his Father
- Now in God's presence, He is our righteousness!

St. Jude 1:24: "Now to Him who is able to keep you from stumbling, and to make you stand in the presence of His glory blameless with great joy." The Other Italians confidently will tell you that their sins have been forgiven by the sacrificial death of Jesus, and now stand before God, RE-DEEMED! There's an old song found in the ancient hymnbooks that sums it all up for them!

Redeemed, redeemed,
Redeemed by the blood of the Lamb,
Redeemed, redeemed,
His child, and forever, I am!

Chapter Five:
Crucifix or Empty Cross?

The Other Italians totally reject the hallowing, devotion and deification of symbols, statues, and religious articles. Interestingly the "Cross" is not an exception! Various art forms depicting it first appeared during the Middle Ages, and artisans from the ninth century on sought to show the suffering of Jesus in realistic and graphic forms; thus the crucifix was created to evidence His suffering.

In the earliest images, the Savior's head is pointed down; His body is contorted and debilitated. The grief and misery of Christ's death by crucifixion became part of the adoration and worship in the Roman Catholic Church. It was during the Reformation, some Catholics reformers rejected the artistic representational and spiritual imagery; yet such continued to be predominantly associated with the Church. The emphasis was to be on the suffering of Christ.

The creation of the Crucifix has no backdrop in the Holy Scriptures. In the early days of the Roman Catholic Church, the Lamb of God was the universal symbol. Interestingly this symbol remained with many of the Reformation groups (i.e.; Moravians), while the Roman Catholic Church held to the orders of the Council of Constantinople in 629 A.D, which ordered: "That, instead of the lamb, our Lord Jesus Christ will be shown hereafter in His human form in images so that we shall be led to remember His mortal life, His passion, and His death, which paid the ransom for mankind."

Again, the focus is on Jesus nailed to a cross and not the empty tomb that signified the resurrection. Remembering the cross is certainly one way to honor the mission of Jesus while on earth but The Other Italians reject it as an item to be worshipped. They recognize the Crucifix as a mirror image of the crucifixion but it is a man-made representation and cannot be sacred outside of the mission it carried out on that fateful day. In reality, it is a remnant of a tree, fashioned in such a way to hang a person for crimes committed.

Reformation Protestants in the 16th century, however, rebelled against the use of the Crucifix and stripped the corpus (body) from the cross, so as to put greater emphasis on the resurrection. Thus, the Crucifix came to be identified specifically with the Roman Catholic Church, the empty cross with the Reformers.

The Other Italians recognize the purpose of Jesus' life was to leave an empty Cross. If He is still memorialized on a 'living cross' where He is depicted as one suffering, the resurrection is shadowed and often left unmentioned. The Other Italians I interviewed said the great danger of worshiping any symbol is that it becomes a substitute for the real thing, the resurrected and living Christ. Those who have left the mother church now cling to the teachings of the Bible, and the memory of an empty wooden cross and empty tomb. They will tell you that they have found a new life for themselves in a living Jesus; one who promised to dwell within the individual and not within a picture or other art form, even one depicting the cross.

Roman Catholics embrace their church with great devotion, and worship the cross and other religious symbols. Several, whom I interviewed, said they "felt close to God" by adoring the symbols. As mentioned, things like the "patron saint" of their village or town continues to link them to their native land; the Crucifix links them to the death of Jesus. These are good reminders, but the actual physical wooden cross on which he died has no spiritual relevance for the living or departed, nor any basis for salvation.

There is beauty in art but the Grace of God is not found in inanimate objects but in a living Lord...Jesus! One can see that the cultural history of the Church runs deep. But culture has no divine substance (power).

Today, the Crucifix is also used in other churches as a symbol of worship. The Orthodox, Eastern Catholic, Coptic, Anglican, Lutheran and other churches all hold to what they believe, is the "spiritual significance" of the crucifix. It continues to be a "religious emblem," and part of the devotion of its members.

While the crucifix is a symbol of Jesus Christ's suffering, The Other Italians focus on the empty cross because they understand suffering was a significant part of His work on earth. But it was not the end all or singular reason why He came. Yes, He had to die! But the cross was empty in a matter of a few hours. His death is no surprise and no miracle; it had been prophesied hundreds and hundreds of years before.

His resurrection is indeed a miracle! It is the act that freed humans from the bondage of sin and death. By coming forth from the grave, Christ Jesus defeated the very last "hold" Satan had on mankind; and that was DEATH, final and without hope!

The Other Italians recognize that with an empty cross they have a crucified Savior; with an empty tomb, they have a "Risen Lord." That is one of the reasons why you'll hear The Other Italians refer to Jesus as LORD. They confess that Jesus is LORD of their lives...living within them.

The Apostle Paul wrote a letter to the church in Galatia and reminded them: "I have been crucified with Christ; and it is no longer I who live, but Christ lives in me; and the life which I now live in the flesh I live by faith in the Son of God, who loved me and gave Himself up for me." (Galatians 2:20) When The Other Italians read the scriptures, they accept its message as if were written directly to them).

While "Good Friday" is remembered, Easter Sunday is celebrated! Without the risen Lord, there is no Christianity, but a good man, who lived and died. Most religions parallel the person and life of Jesus to their own religious founder and leader. But the comparison stops there! "Good men and women" have appeared throughout the centuries and tried to teach the virtues of righteous living. BUT ONLY ONE CAME FORTH FROM THE GRAVE…Jesus of Nazareth, the Son of God!

My research revealed that early on, Christian theology saw the Crucifix as a form of idolatry. The Biblical admonition, "Thou shalt not make unto thee any graven image," (Exodus 20:4-6) was taken literally. Theologians understood the scriptures to mean one was not to create or make any image as an item to be worshipped, adored or revered. Symbols were seen as a substitute for the "spiritual reality" that came with salvation. The Other Italians no longer "bless" (Genuflect) themselves before a statue or relief because Christ is not in an object, but living in their heart!

Nowhere in the New Testament Church were there statues to worship, memorialize, or created to depict the life of Christ. The Other Italians express they have no need to see, hear or touch something to know the reality of Christ in their lives. No reminder is needed, and nothing could substitute or be used in place of the risen Lord living, and seeing Him revealed in the scriptures. When Jesus finally gave His life as a ransom for mankind's sin, no symbols would ever be necessary again to acknowledge the presence of God on earth. Jesus came to fill the ultimate void in every man and woman's life! He is a living symbol!

In most Roman Catholic churches and cathedrals one will find a larger than life Crucifix, while in Christian churches there is an obvious absence of Christ on the Cross. Usually an empty cross appears above the altar. The word "Crucifix" comes from the Latin and means "one fixed to a cross."

The Other Italians have taken Him down both mentally and physically, and accept the scriptures that declare He lives within the regenerated individual, not without, in or on something! To them, the RESURECTION is the fulfillment of the life and redemptive work of Jesus. Roman Catholics, while acknowledging this, still hold to the images of Christ on the cross. The fact is that from the time Jesus was taken down from the cross it never again held His body. They accept this and do not clutch to a symbol as they see the body of Jesus many steps beyond this memorial. He was taken to a tomb, rose from the dead, appeared to numerous individuals and groups of people numbering over 500, ascended into heaven, and by faith they see Him descending in His "second coming."

Note: The Catechism of the Catholic Church acknowledges this sequence: "The faith of the first community of believers is based on the witness of concrete men known to the Christians and for the most part still living among them. Peter and the Twelve are the primary "witnesses to his Resurrection," but they are not the only ones - Paul speaks clearly of more than five hundred persons to whom Jesus appeared on a single occasion and also of James and of all the apostles." (502) - (Part-One: Profession of Faith).

My surveys indicate that few individuals know that after His death and resurrection, Jesus appeared to more people than just the Disciples in a room in Jerusalem.

Christianity is about the finished work of the cross and not about what we can do to attain God's favor. There is no "doing" in Christ...for it is already done! The Crucifixion occurred one time! St. Peter said this (1 Peter 1:3-4 & 18): "Blessed be the God and Father of our Lord Jesus Christ, who according to His great mercy has caused us to be born again to a living hope through the resurrection of Jesus Christ from the dead, to obtain an inheritance which is imperishable and undefiled and will not fade away, reserved in heaven for you. For Christ also died for sins once for all, the just for the unjust, so that He might bring us to God, having been put to death in the flesh, but made alive in the spirit!"

For Italians, coming from Roman Catholic teaching, this is not foreign, but they say it was never internalized or understood as being complete and finished. They told this author they were always trying to do something to attain God's forgiveness. Basic to this was their obedience to their Church. They expressed the problem of trying to be good always left them wondering if they were good enough. At that point many said they just gave up or tried to negotiate their salvation.

Down through the ages men and women have endeavored to bargain with God: "God, I'll do something for you if you'll do this for me!" The never-ending quest for His grace was exactly that, never ending! Much of the worship of symbols in the Roman Catholic Church are viewed by The Other Italians as an effort to appease God or try to earn His grace. They confessed they were always trying to do the right thing when it came to their "religious behavior." Six days a week they lived their lives according to culture and tradition, yet on in church they demonstrated their religious posture. As humans we can't imagine God doing something, doing it once and giving us the benefit for eternity! St Peter spoke in the book of Acts about trying to buy favor with God: "But Peter said to him, "May your silver perish with you, because you thought you could obtain the gift of God with money." (Acts 8:20)

With all the personal obligatory devotion (Obligations are part of the religious regiment of the Roman Catholic Church) to the cross, many people can't see beyond the rotting wood, spikes and bloodstains. Of course, today ornamental crosses are made of various materials from ornate wood to precious gold. For many it is an historic symbol and nothing more. The Other Italians said wearing a cross in their former days, made them feel religious.

But there is one scripture that does seem to imply that the cross might have some significance in the plan of God for mankind's worship to Him. The Apostle Paul wrote a letter to the congregation in Galatia (Galatians 6:14): "But may it never be that I would boast, except in the cross of our Lord Jesus Christ, through which the world has been crucified to me, and I to the world."

Taken literally one might be convinced that the Apostle was suggesting the cross should be worshipped. But he wasn't! Reading the accompanying scriptures around this particular verse (its context) indicates Paul wanted his listeners to know that there was nothing outside of the sacrificial death of Jesus that meant anything to him. In fact, his writings throughout the New Testament indicate he possessed an aversion to anything that anyone would or could add to the ministry and death of Jesus. He warned against this! The Apostle Paul understood the cross for what it was! Keep in mind he lived during the Roman rule and was quite familiar with death by crucifixion.

A BIT OF HISTORY REGARDING THE ROMAN CROSS

In ancient Rome the cross was an instrument of death. It was made of wood and designed to inflict a slow, torturous death. A crucifixion would produce a death with an unbearable degree of suffering and pain. One must keep in mind that the cross did not save anyone in any spiritual sense. It was the ultimate end to a person's life. Even though Jesus suffered death on a cross, that specific cross was not sanctified or made holy.

If we think of the cross in the sense of it being consecrated or hallowed it becomes an idol in and of itself! In no way did it glorify, nor did God glorify it. The cross was a device that was employed for the sole purpose of execution. The God-hating Romans loved its potential. If they didn't enjoy its merits they would have used some other means of death for their enemies. Because of the size of their kingdom, with its far-reaching borders, the cross was the most inhumane means of capital punishment. A citizen or traveler in Rome would think twice about leading a rebellion against the government.

When Jesus was removed from the cross, it did not change its form or meaning. There is nothing sacred about it. In fact, because it cost a lot of money to produce, most likely the cross upon which Jesus died was used after...again and again. It was not the cross that glorified God...it was the Glorified One who died on it!

The scriptures are the only source The Other Italians find creditable in the matter of understanding the significance of the crucifixion! It is the empty tomb that confirms His ultimate mission. St Paul wrote this in his letter to the Church in Corinth: "and if Christ has not been raised, then our preaching is vain, your faith also is vain!" (1 Corinthians 15:14)

The Catechism of the Roman Catholic Church places great emphasis on the acknowledgement and worship of physical symbols: "1192 Sacred images in our churches and homes are intended to awaken and nourish our faith in the mystery of Christ." (Part two-Celebration of the Christian Mystery)

The Other Italians believe the scriptures are as relevant today as they were when written. They believe the content of the scriptures was given for their "awakening and nourishment," which is promised therein! St Mark wrote: "...be a good servant of Christ Jesus, constantly <u>nourished</u> on the words of the faith and of the sound doctrine which you have been following." (I Timothy 4:6)

Romans 10:17 reads: "So faith comes from hearing, and hearing by the word of Christ!" It is the testimony of The Other Italians that they remain steadfast in their faith by the power of the God's Holy Spirit in their lives, and the assurance He will illumine the scriptures! Symbols, statues and other religious articles play no part in their worship or faith.

Chapter Six:
Grand Cathedral or Rented Gymnasium?

The magnificent cathedrals erected all over the world are an enduring witness to great architecture and the sacrifice of many people. The irony and tragedy is that many of these great "temples of worship," constructed during the Middle Ages, were known to have been built on the backs of the oppressed. In some respects, the Middle Ages were indeed "spiritually dark!"

The association and practices of the Roman Catholic Church, which had aligned itself with the political schema of the period, also come into question during this era. Not necessarily for what it did…as much as what it failed to do.

From the period of 590 to 1517, the Church dominated and controlled religion, philosophy, moral codes, politics, arts and education and more! Many scholars do consider this period to be a darkened time for Christianity in the world as basic Biblical theology, believed and practiced heretofore, literally disappeared. Theological depravity permitted corruption that led to horrible actions.

The Medieval Church played a far greater role in the lives of the people then it does today. During that time, the Church in Rome established an ordered routine for the daily life of the individual. Doctrinally, peasants believed in both heaven and hell and were told they could only attain heaven through obedience to the Church. They existed in a state of bondage. The idea of a better place kept them faithful to their ecclesiastical teachings and daily work. In reality, a combination of fear and hope controlled their psyche.

Peasants worked for free on Church land at the expense of their own farming. The emotionally overpowering message to them was that the Church determined whether they would go to heaven or hell. Fear of retribution kept them servants of the church. Who would argue or rebel knowing the consequences?

They were obliged to pay a tax of ten percent (or tithe) of what they earned in a given year to the Church. Tithes could be paid in either money or in goods produced by the peasant farmers. As peasants had little money most paid in seeds, harvested grain and animals. What the Church received was stored in tithe barns. They were told that a failure to pay tithes would result in their souls going to Hell after they had died. The outcome of all of this was a pervading fear of what would happen to them if they did not work for, and obey the Church. The end the result was the construction of many magnificent Cathedrals we still have today. They are indeed beautiful, but The Other Italians do not view or revere them in any spiritual sense.

For most people it is logical to ask these kinds of questions: Is there a place on this earth where one can feel the undeniable presence of God? Are there places to worship that are more "sacred" or "blessed?" Where is the place of true worship…temple or Tee Pee?

The Other Italians refer to the scriptures for guidance in the matter of a place to worship God. Remember the Apostle Paul's message to the Greeks? "The God who made the world and everything in it is the Lord of heaven and earth and does not live in temples built by human hands." (Acts 17:24)

The Bible records an important event that answers this question. The answer comes directly from Jesus. It is one that can easily clarify where and how to worship.

Perceiving that Jesus was "Godly," and might have the answer to some of her religious questions, a woman who lived in Samaria, asked Him that same question: Where should a person worship? Here is the account and His answer to her question. We find the incident in St. John's Gospel chapter 4 verses 19-26:

"The woman said to Him, "Sir, I perceive that You are a prophet. Our fathers worshiped in this mountain, and you people say that in Jerusalem is the place where men ought to worship." Jesus said to her, "Woman, believe Me, an hour is coming when neither in this mountain nor in Jerusalem will you worship the Father. You worship what you do not know; we worship what we know, for salvation is from the Jews. But an hour is coming, and now is, when the true worshipers will worship the Father in spirit and truth; for such people the Father seeks to be His worshipers. <u>God is spirit</u>, and those who worship Him must worship in spirit and truth." The woman *said to Him, "I know that Messiah is coming (He who is called Christ); when that One comes, He will declare all things to us." Jesus said to her, "I who speak to you am He."

The Other Italians do not believe you find God in a building, no matter how magnificent the structural design may be. There is no argument that beautiful, ornate architecture can inspire an individual. But God's presence is spiritual and cannot be confined to a structure, mountaintop, majestic landscape or any other beautiful thing.

The Other Italians accept God's grace as a constant in their lives, and not "enhanced" by anything, including brick and stone. They do not believe He dwells in an art form or statue. Jesus confirms this when He answers her: "<u>God is spirit!</u>" Thus an individual's relationship with God is not temporal (terrestrial or earthly), but exactly that…spiritual! While one can express his or her love in words that can be understood, it is heart to heart communication that God understands. The Other Italians identify it as a consecrated life to the Lordship of Jesus; one where communion with God is evident.

They reason if there is a place where God is present, what happens to the individual when he or she is not in that place - whether it's a magnificent cathedral or some historic site associated with the life, death and resurrection of Jesus. Some people actually erect altars in their house; but what happens when they are at the supermarket, on a bus or on a cruise ship?

In the book of Samuel we read: 1 Samuel 16:7: "God sees not as man sees, for man looks at the outward appearance, but the Lord looks at the heart." The Other Italians see their relationship with God as a "heart to heart" – spiritual relationship.

The question asked by "the woman at the well" is not new! Down through the ages people have sought a place, a time and a mood to feel the presence of God. Some travel thousands of miles to memorials, cities, mountains and the like. This whole issue is what makes the ministry of Jesus so profound. The Bible assures us that Jesus meets people where they are…in their home, by a poolside, on a mountaintop, in the streets and yes, in a beautiful house of worship! And He communicates with them spiritually through His written word. The Other Italians recognize the scriptures as the "mind of God!" Men and women have actually discovered Him for themselves in a prison cell and even on a cruise ship! He speaks to the heart!

The church structure certainly can be respected and admired for its physical beauty but The Other Italians believe the presence of God is not to be found within any structure. St Matthew wrote: "…where two or three are gathered together in my name, there I am in their midst." (Matthew 18:20)

As for identifying any particular place possessing a more spiritual ambiance to pray and worship God, one needs only look at the scriptures for the answer. God's presence is just as evident in your backyard or in the seat of a city taxicab!

The Other Italians accept the promise that God is everywhere, waiting for men and women to call upon Him! Here is a simple illustration that humorously describes the "presence of God" in a person's life:

THE PRAYER OF CYRUS BROWN

"The proper way for a man to pray," Said Deacon Lemuel Keyes, "And the only proper attitude Is down upon his knees." "No, I should say the way to pray,"   Said Rev. Doctor Wise, "Is standing straight with outstretched arms And rapt and upturned eyes." "Oh, no; no, no," said Elder Slow, "Such posture is too proud: A man should pray with eyes fast closed

And head contritely bowed." "It seems to me his hands should be Aus-
terely clasped in front. With both thumbs pointing toward the ground,"
Said Rev. Doctor Blunt. "Las' year I fell in Hodgkin's well Head first," said
Cyrus Brown, "With both my heels a-stickin' up, My head a-pinting
down; An' I made a prayer right then an' there—best prayer I ever said,
The prayingest prayer I ever prayed, A-standing on my head."

The Other Italians think of the unfounded restrictions individuals put
upon themselves if they limit God's presence to a place or time. They do
not believe one has to enter the halls of a great temple to realize the presence
of God.

HOW DO YOU COMMUNICATE WITH GOD?

Consider this explanation in light of what the Holy Scriptures say.
While we can converse with a friend here on earth in human terms, gestures
and facial expressions; communion with God is, (as Jesus explained to the
woman at the well), spiritual…"Heart to Heart." Yet, even that falls short
understanding what it means to be in the presence of God. It certainly is
not limited to the Grand Cathedrals of yesteryear!

The Other Italians believe the life-long relationship and dialogue with
God begins with a prayer like this: "I know I am a sinner, and I ask for your
forgiveness. I believe you died for my sins and rose from the dead. I now
purpose to trust you and will follow you as my Lord and Savior. Guide my
life and help me to do your will. I pray this prayer in the name of Jesus!
Amen!" (Some call this "The Sinner's Prayer)

One of the most difficult things The Other Italians had to face was the
whole idea of communicating with God with their spirit. In their former
religious state, they said they chanted, gestured, touched and practiced "rote
monologues" to communicate with God. They knew what the word "spiritual" meant, but couldn't grasp the how they could commune with Him
outside of being emotionally stimulated by something said or something
they could see, hear and touch. They had been taught that God is in things.
The idea of living in a person needed some explaining.

WRITTEN ON STONE OR ON THE HEART?

If we look back to the time when God gave Moses the Ten Commandments, we can visualize two tablets of stone clutched in his hands. Written on them were the Laws of God! The Ten Commandments are the very foundation for every law governing mankind! While they were once engraved in stone, Jesus says, they are now in the heart of the believer. One converted Italian whom I interviewed said, "Christ Jesus is my Lord…the living reality of all that God planned for me! Although I used to think I kept the Ten Commandments, and that would save me, I came to learn that no one has ever kept them except Jesus. I realized that I was incapable of keeping them; but the spirit of Christ has implanted them within me, and I yield and conform to them. I know when I'm doing right and I know when I'm doing wrong!"

St. Paul wrote this to the Church in Corinth: "But the one who joins himself to the Lord is one spirit with Him."(1 Cor. 6:17)

The Other Italians are aware of the character of God as described in the Bible and understand that He cannot communicate with sin. Sin is the great "separator." Jesus came to take that sin and make it possible to enter into the very presence of God…to have that "spiritual communion." The Other Italians have accepted this as the foundation of their faith and recognize that He is ever present in their lives. They have become one with Christ Jesus…united forever!

Romans 10:13 sums up God's provision for all of mankind: "for "Whoever will call on the name of the Lord will be saved." There are no other alliances, associations, memberships, unions, connections or any other means of acquiring God's forgiving and saving grace.

And, as for the question, where to worship? Here's the Biblical answer: "However, the Most High does not dwell in houses made by human hands;" Acts 7:48

"The God who made the world and all things in it, since He is Lord of heaven and earth, does not dwell in temples made with hands!" Acts 17:24

The Other Italians will tell you the relationship they have with God is not a "brain thing." That is, it even surpasses the intellectual idea of communication as described in a letter from St. Paul to the believers in Ephesus:

"For this reason I bow my knees before the Father, from whom every family in heaven and on earth derives its name that He would grant you, according to the riches of His glory, to be strengthened with power through His Spirit in the inner man, so that Christ may dwell in your hearts through faith; and that you, being rooted and grounded in love, may be able to comprehend with all the saints what is the breadth and length and height and depth, and to know the love of Christ which surpasses knowledge, that you may be filled up to all the fullness of God." (Eph. 3:13-19)

Here's that portion of scripture in the Living Bible translation: "When I think of the wisdom and scope of his plan, I fall down on my knees and pray to the Father of all the great family of God some of them already in heaven and some down here on earth that out of his glorious, unlimited resources He will give you the mighty inner strengthening of his Holy Spirit. And I pray that Christ will be more and more at home in your hearts, living within you as you trust in Him. May your roots go down deep into the soil of God's marvelous love; and may you be able to feel and understand, as all God's children should, how long, how wide, how deep, and how high his love really is; and to experience this love for yourselves, though it is so great that you will never see the end of it or fully know or understand it. And so at last you will be filled up with God himself."

Chapter Seven:
The Crucifixion of Jesus:
A Temporary or Final Sacrifice?

In light of the differences between Roman Catholicism and what The Other Italians believe, a vital question arises regarding the crucifixion of Jesus: Was it a one-time occurrence or does it have to be repeated in ceremony or sacrament to attain God's forgiveness?

The core belief of Roman Catholicism is that the Mass is the principal means of receiving God's saving grace. For the parishioner it is a ritual that he or she may participate in hundreds, even thousands of times during their lifetime, while The Other Italians believe that Jesus died "once and for all." St. Peter declared this: "For Christ also died for sins once for all, the just for the unjust, so that He might bring us to God, having been put to death in the flesh, but made alive in the spirit;" (1Peter 3:18)

It is the record of the scriptures that says Jesus died one time, and no Biblical explanation, admonition or directive is written or inferenced indicating otherwise. This is the overwhelming issue when contrasting the beliefs of The Other Italians and Roman Catholic doctrine. It is an irreconcilable difference! To fully understand the conflict in theology is to explore the reason why Jesus had to die in the first place. We start with the topic of sin.

THE CONSEQUENCES OF SIN

The Apostle Paul's message to the Church in Rome summarized the state of sin in just few words: (Romans 5:12 "Therefore, just as through one man (Adam) sin entered into the world, and death through sin, and so death spread to all men, because all sinned." (Note: There are no exceptions in the scriptures. No one ever received a "pass" from the curse of sin and the judgment thereof). Of course after Adam and Eve sinned they didn't die immediately ("death through sin"). The Biblical record implies they lived very long lives. So what died? They died spiritually, and that meant separation from their Creator. That first couple lost their spiritual union with God, and everyone since has needed to be reconciled to Him. But there was a promise that came with the expulsion from the Garden of Eden; God pledged He'd bring humans back into fellowship with Himself. He did not announce that Adam or Eve had to do something to "make amends." The message to them was that He would do something through them...their seed, and it would be a one-time occurrence. A relationship between God and Man could be restored, and a plan for redemption was announced. It centered on the destruction of Satan...the "tempter." The temptation of Adam and Eve came from without...the serpent, Satan. Their sin brought about our sin nature.

With the understanding that Adam and Eve died spiritually, there would now be the need for a "rebirth" of the spirit within all who have ever lived. Jesus explained this to Nicodemus when He said, "You must be born again!"

The Bible records the fall of an angel named, "Lucifer," who went into rebellion against God, and has since been committed to holding captive His creation.

The Apostle Paul explained the dire consequences of his "captive trap" to Timothy when he shared advice as to how to teach and treat those he would minister to in the future: "...and they may come to their senses and escape from the snare of the devil, having been held captive by him to do his will." (2 Timothy 2:26)

The pledge God made to Adam and Eve is that God's Champion, the "perfect, sinless, son of man" would trample Satan underfoot. It would not be man's battle for if it were, Satan would be the winner! The account of the fall of mankind is recorded in the first chapters of Genesis, and the assurance (guarantee) of redemption is there too!

The promise of deliverance is the central theme of the entire Old Testament. As incredible as it may seem, thousands of years before Jesus walked up Golgotha Hill to the cross, the Holy Spirit moved upon the prophets to write things they knew nothing about at the time. What they foretold were the events surrounding Jesus' birth, life, death and resurrection. His one time sacrificial death on the cross was absolutely necessary in the plan for mankind. But until Jesus would come and atone for their sin, God instituted a plan where a continuous sacrifice was to be offered. The Old Testament tells of the ritual sacrifice Priests carried out by offering an unspotted lamb on an altar.

Consider these prophecies that were made hundreds and hundreds of years before their occurrence. They reveal the very explicit details of the "ultimate and final sacrifice" that would occur to bring mankind back into fellowship with God.

HIS BIRTH WAS FORETOLD

Typical of the prophesies concerning the birth of Jesus are these:

Isaiah 7:14—Isaiah prophesies that a pure young woman will give birth to God's Son.

- Matthew 1:18–23—Isaiah's prophecy is fulfilled.
- Isaiah 9:6—Isaiah prophesies that Jesus Christ will come as a baby; Jesus is described by several names.
- Micah 5:2—Micah prophesies that Jesus will be born in Bethlehem.
- Matthew 2:4-6-The scribes knew that Bethlehem was the prophesied birthplace of the Messiah. Luke 2:4-7 - Jesus is born. (The title, Messiah, literally means the "Spirit of God.")

The Prophet Isaiah wrote: "His name shall be called Wonderful Counselor, The mighty God, The everlasting Father, The Prince of Peace!" Isaiah 9:6)

THE NECESSITY OF THE CRUCIFIXION

On the day of the Lord's crucifixion, every prophecy detailing it was fulfilled. Only Jesus fulfilled them, proving He was the Messiah that was spoken of in the Old Testament.

These prophecies begin in the book of Genesis. They commence with the promise to Adam and Eve that the evil one would be destroyed. Jesus would defeat Satan, known as the… "Prince of the world."

St. Paul's letter to the Ephesians spells it out for us: "Once you were under God's curse, doomed forever for your sins. You went along with the crowd and were just like all the others, full of sin, obeying Satan, the mighty prince of the power of the air, who is at work right now in the hearts of those who are against the Lord. All of us used to be just as they are, our lives expressing the evil within us, doing every wicked thing that our passions or our evil thoughts might lead us into. We started out bad, being born with evil natures, and were under God's anger just like everyone else. But God is so rich in mercy; he loved us so much that even though we were spiritually dead and doomed by our sins, he gave us back our lives again[a] when he raised Christ from the dead—only by his undeserved favor have we ever been saved." (Ephesians 2:1-5 LB)

The Other Italians also hold to these words: "Finally, be strong in the Lord and in the strength of His might. Put on the full armor of God, so that you will be able to stand firm against the schemes of the devil. For our struggle is not against flesh and blood, but against the rulers, against the powers, against the world forces of this darkness, against the spiritual forces of wickedness in the heavenly places."(Ephesians 6:10-12)

Let's look at the prophecies, and the proof of their fulfillment! (Note: The prophecies are found in the Old Testament and their fulfillment in the New Testament):

THE BETRAYAL OF JESUS WAS FORETOLD

Prophesy: "Even my close friend in whom I trusted, who ate my bread, Has lifted up his heel against me Even a man, my close friend in whom I trusted, who ate of my bread, has lifted up his heel against me." (Psalm 41:9)

Fulfillment: "Then Judas Iscariot, who was one of the twelve, went off to the chief priests in order to betray Him to them. They were glad when they heard this, and promised to give him money. And he began seeking how to betray Him at an opportune time." (Mark 14:10-11)

THE DISCIPLES WOULD FORESAKE JESUS

Prophesy: "Awake, O sword, against My Shepherd, and against the man, My Associate, Declares the Lord of hosts. Strike the Shepherd that the sheep may be scattered; And I will turn My hand against the little ones." (Zechariah. 13:7)

Fulfillment: "And they all left Him and fled." (Mark 14:50)

THE PRICE OF BETRAYAL IS FORETOLD

Prophesy: "I said to them, "If it is good in your sight, give me my wages; but if not, never mind!" So they weighed out thirty shekels of silver as my wages." (Zechariah. 11:12)

Fulfillment: "…and said, What are you willing to give me to betray Him to you?" And they weighed out thirty pieces of silver to him." (Matthew 26:15)

WHERE THE BETRAYAL MONEY WAS TO GO

Prophesy: "Then the Lord said to me, "Throw it to the potter, that magnificent price at which I was valued by them." So I took the thirty shekels of silver and threw them to the potter in the house of the Lord." (Zechariah 11:13)

Fulfillment: "Then when Judas, who had betrayed Him, saw that He had been condemned, he felt remorse and returned the thirty pieces of silver to the chief priests and elders, saying, "I have sinned by betraying innocent blood." But they said, "What is that to us? See to that yourself!" And he threw the pieces of silver into the temple sanctuary and departed; and he went away and hanged himself. The chief priests took the pieces of silver and said, "It is not lawful to put them into the temple treasury, since it is the price of blood." And they conferred together and with the money bought the Potter's Field as a burial place for strangers." (Matthew 27:3-7)

THE PROPHET ISAIAH PREDICTED JESUS WOULD BE THE SACRIFICAL PASSOVER LAMB TO BE SLAUGHTERED TO MAKE ATONEMENT FOR THE SINS OF MANKIND

Prophesy: "He was oppressed and He was afflicted, Yet He did not open His mouth; Like a lamb that is led to slaughter, And like a sheep that is silent before its shearers, So He did not open His mouth. He is brought as a lamb to the slaughter..." (Isaiah 53:7)

Fulfillment: "Clean out the old leaven so that you may be a new lump, just as you are in fact unleavened. For Christ our Passover also has been sacrificed." (I Corinthians 5:7)

"Knowing that you were not redeemed with perishable things like silver or gold from your futile way of life inherited from your forefathers, but with precious blood, as of a lamb unblemished and spotless, the blood of Christ. For He was foreknown before the foundation of the world, but has appeared in these last times for the sake of you." (I Peter. 1:18-20)

JESUS TO BE SCOURGED AND MOCKED

Prophesy: "I gave My back to those who strike Me, And My cheeks to those who pluck out the beard; I did not cover My face from humiliation and spitting." (Isaiah 50:6)

Fulfillment: "Then he released Barabbas for them; but after having Jesus scourged, he handed Him over to be crucified. Then the soldiers of the governor took Jesus into the Praetorium and gathered the whole Roman cohort around Him. They stripped Him and put a scarlet robe on Him. And after twisting together a crown of thorns, they put it on His head, and a reed in His right hand; and they knelt down before Him and mocked Him, saying, "Hail, King of the Jews!" They spat on Him, and took the reed and began to beat Him on the head." (Matthew 27:26-30)

THE BODY OF JESUS WOULD BE INJURED

Prophesy: "Just as many were astonished at you, My people, So His appearance was marred more than any man And His form more than the sons of men." (Isaiah 52:14)

"I can count all my bones. They look, they stare at me." (Psalm 22:17)

Fulfillment: "Wishing to satisfy the crowd, Pilate released Barabbas for them, and after having Jesus scourged, he handed Him over to be crucified."(Mark 15:15)

"Pilate then took Jesus and scourged Him." (John 19:1)

HE'D BE SHAMED AND DISHONORED

Prophesy: "For zeal for Your house has consumed me, And the reproaches of those who reproach You have fallen on me." (Psalms 69:9)

"You know my reproach and my shame and my dishonor; All my adversaries are before You. Reproach has broken my heart and I am so sick. And I looked for sympathy, but there was none, And for comforters, but I found none." (Psalms 69:19-20)

Fulfillment: "At that time Jesus said to the crowds, Have you come out with swords and clubs to arrest Me as you would against a robber?" (Matt. 26:55)

"What do you think?" they answered, "He deserves death!" (Matt. 26:66)

FALSE WITNESSES WOULD ACCUSE HIM

Prophesy: "Malicious witnesses rise up; They ask me of things that I do not know." (Psalms. 35:11)

Fulfillment: "Now the chief priests and the whole Council kept trying to obtain testimony against Jesus to put Him to death, and they were not finding any. For many were giving false testimony against Him but their testimony was not consistent. Some stood up and began to give false testimony against Him…" (Mark 14:55-57)

JESUS WOULD'NT RISE UP TO DEFEND HIMSELF

Prophesy: "He was oppressed and He was afflicted, Yet He did not open His mouth; Like a lamb that is led to slaughter, And like a sheep that is silent before its shearers, So He did not open His mouth." (Isaiah 53:7)

Fulfillment: "Then Pilate *said to Him, "Do You not hear how many things they testify against You?" And He did not answer him with regard to even a single charge, so the governor was quite amazed." (Matthew 27:13-14)

THAT JESUS WOULD BE A "SIN OFFERING" FOR MANKIND IS TOLD IN VIVID DETAIL – INCLUDING THE STRIPES THAT WOULD BE INFLICTED AND MORE

Prophesy: "Surely our grief He Himself bore, and our sorrows He carried; Yet we ourselves esteemed Him stricken, Smitten of God, and afflicted. But He was pierced through for our transgressions, He was crushed for our iniquities; The chastening for our well-being fell upon Him, And by His scourging we are healed .All of us like sheep have gone astray, Each of us has turned to his own way; But the Lord has caused the iniquity of us all To fall on Him." But the Lord was pleased. To crush Him, putting Him to grief; If He would render Himself as a guilt offering, He will see His offspring, He will prolong His days, And the good pleasure of the Lord will prosper in His hand. As a result of the anguish of His soul, He will see it and be satisfied; By His knowledge the Righteous One, My Servant, will justify the many, As He will bear their iniquities."(Isaiah 53:4-6, 10-11)

Fulfillment: "So he then handed Him over to them to be crucified. They took Jesus, therefore, and He went out, bearing His own cross, to the place called the Place of a Skull, which is called in Hebrew, Golgotha. There they crucified Him, and with Him two other men, one on either side, and Jesus in between. Pilate also wrote an inscription and put it on the cross. It was written, "JESUS THE NAZARENE, THE KING OF THE JEWS." (John 19:16-19)

JESUS WOULD BE TREATED LIKE A COMMON THIEF AND NUMBERED WITH CRIMINALS

Prophesy: "Therefore, I will allot Him a portion with the great, And He will divide the booty with the strong; Because He poured out Himself to death, And was numbered with the transgressors; Yet He Himself bore the sin of many, And interceded for the transgressors." (Isa. 53:12).

Fulfillment: "Two others also, who were criminals, were being led away to be put to death with Him. When they came to the place called, The Skull; there they crucified Him and the criminals, one on the right and the other on the left." (Luke 23:32-33)

HIS HANDS AND FEET WOULD BE PIERCED

Prophesy: "For dogs have surrounded me; A band of evildoers has encompassed me; They pierced my hands and my feet." (Psalms. 22:16)

Fulfillment: "It was the third hour when they crucified Him." (Mark 15:25)

"So the other disciples were saying to him, "We have seen the Lord!" But he said to them, "Unless I see in His hands the imprint of the nails, and put my finger into the place of the nails, and put my hand into His side, I will not believe. After eight days His disciples were again inside, and Thomas with them. Jesus *came, the doors having been shut, and stood in their midst and said, "Peace be with you." Then He *said to Thomas, "Reach here with your finger, and see My hands; and reach here your hand and put it into My side; and do not be unbelieving, but believing." (John 20:25-27)

HIS GARMENTS WOULD BE PARTED OUT

Prophesy: "They divide my garments among them, and for my clothing they cast lots." (Psalms 22:18)

Fulfillment: "So they said to one another, "Let us not tear it, but cast lots for it, to decide whose it shall be"; this was to fulfill the Scripture: "They divided My outer garments among them, and for My clothing they cast lots." (John 19:24)

HE WOULD BE GIVEN VINEGAR TO DRINK

Prophesy: "They also gave me gall for my food; And for my thirst they gave me vinegar to drink." (Psalms 69:21)

Fulfillment: "they gave Him wine to drink mixed with gall; and after tasting it, He was unwilling to drink." (Matt. 27:34)

MANY WOULD WITNESS HIS CRUCIFIXION

Prophesy: "I can count all my bones. They look, they stare at me;" (Psalms 22:17)

Fulfillment: "And sitting down, they began to keep watch over Him there." (Matt.27:36) "And all the crowds who came together for this spectacle, when they observed what had happened, began to return, beating their breasts." (Luke 23:48)

HIS FAMILY AND FRIENDS WOULD WITNESS HIS CRUCIFIXION

Prophesy: "My loved ones and my friends stand aloof from my plague; And my kinsmen stand afar off."(Psalms 38:11)

Fulfillment: "And all His acquaintances and the women who accompanied Him from Galilee were standing at a distance, seeing these things." (Luke 23:49)

ON-LOOKERS WOULD SHAKE THEIR HEAD AT THE SCENE

Prophesy: "I also have become a reproach to them; When they see me, they wag their head." (Psalms 109:25)

Fulfillment: "And those passing by were hurling abuse at Him, wagging their heads!" (Matt. 27:39-4)

PEOPLE WOULD RIDCULE HIM AT THE CROSS

Prophesy: "Commit yourself to the Lord; let Him deliver him; Let Him rescue him, because He delights in him." (Psalms 22:8).

Fulfillment: "He trusts in God; let God rescue Him now, if He delights in Him; for He said, 'I am the Son of God.' The robbers who had been crucified with Him were also insulting Him with the same words." (Matthew 27:43-44)

HE WOULD PRAY FOR SINNERS WHILE BEING CRUCIFIED

Prophesy: "And was numbered with the transgressors; Yet, He Himself bore the sin of many, And interceded for the transgressors." (Isaiah 53:12)

Fulfillment: "But Jesus was saying, "Father, forgive them; for they do not know what they are doing." And they cast lots, dividing up His garments among themselves." (Luke 23:34)

SOLDIERS WOULD CAST LOTS FOR HIS CLOTHING

Prophesy: "They divide my garments among them, And for my clothing they cast lots." (Psalm 22:18)

Fulfillment: "And they cast lots, dividing up His garments among themselves." (Luke 23:34)

THE FINAL THOUGHTS OF JESUS

Prophecy: "My God, my God, why have You forsaken me? Far from my deliverance are the words of my groaning?" (Psalm 22:1)

Fulfillment: "About the ninth hour Jesus cried out with a loud voice, saying, "Eli, Eli, lama sabachthani?" that is, "My God, My God, why have You forsaken Me?" (Matthew 27:46)

BODY WOULD BE PIERCED WITH A SPEAR

Prophesy: "I will pour out on the house of David and on the inhabitants of Jerusalem, the Spirit of grace and of supplication, so that they will look on Me whom they have pierced;" (Zechariah. 12:10)

Fulfillment: "But one of the soldiers pierced His side with a spear;"(John 19:34, 37)

JESUS WOULD COMMIT HIS SPIRIT TO GOD

Prophesy: "Into Your hand I commit my spirit; You have ransomed me, Lord, God of truth." (Psalm 31:5)

Fulfillment: "And Jesus, crying out with a loud voice, said, "Father, into Your hands I commit My spirit." Having said this, He breathed His last. And after crying out with a loud voice, Jesus said, 'Father, into Your hands

I commit My spirit.' And when He had said these things, He expired," (Luke 23:46)

DAVID PROPHESIED THE LAST WORDS OF JESUS

Prophesy: "My God, my God, why have You forsaken me?" (Psalm 22:1)

Fulfillment: "Now from the sixth hour darkness fell upon all the land until the ninth hour. About the ninth hour Jesus cried out with a loud voice, saying, "Eli, Eli, lama sabachthani?" that is, "My God, My God, why have You forsaken Me?" (Matthew 17:46)

NONE OF HIS BONES WOULD BE BROKEN The bones of the victim were usually broken to hasten death)

Prophesy: "He keeps all his bones; not one of them is broken." (Psalm 34:20)

Fulfillment: "So the soldiers came, and broke the legs of the first man and of the other who was crucified with Him; but coming to Jesus, when they saw that He was already dead, they did not break His legs." (John 19:32-33)

HE'D BE BURIED IN A RICH MAN'S TOMB

Prophesy: "His grave was assigned with wicked men, Yet He was with a rich man in His death, Because He had done no violence, Nor was there any deceit in His mouth." (Isaiah 53:9)

Fulfillment: "When it was evening, there came a rich man from Arimathea, named Joseph, who himself had also become a disciple of Jesus. This man went to Pilate and asked for the body of Jesus. Then Pilate ordered it to be given to him. And Joseph took the body and wrapped it in a clean linen cloth, and laid it in his own new tomb, which he had hewn out in the rock; and he rolled a large stone against the entrance of the tomb and went away." (Matthew. 27:57-60)

ST. MATTHEW SUMS UP THE PROPHECIES WITH THE WORDS OF AN "EYEWITNESS"

"Now when the centurion, and they that were with him, watching Jesus, saw the earthquake, and those things that were done, they feared greatly, saying, Truly, this was the Son of God." (Matthew 27:54)

Sound familiar? This is the declaration St. Peter made when Jesus asked: "Who do you say that I am?"

Jesus came to the earth, fulfilling every prophecy within the Old Testament for one purpose, and it is recorded in the Book of St. John 3:1: "For God sent not his Son into the world to condemn the world; but that the world through Him might be saved."

The Old Testament reports on the lives of individuals and nations; that from the very beginning men and women have been searching for the "Divine" in some form…somewhere. There has been an ongoing search of the heavens and earth and beneath. Little did know what they were searching for, would one day he'd be born of a virgin, live a sinless life, die on a cross and come forth from His grave!

You'll remember St. Paul's encounter with the Greeks. (Acts 17: 16-34) He told the Athenians that their "Unknown God" is Jesus! The Other Italians recognize the promise that was announced in the Garden of Eden, and the prophesies throughout the Bible. They will tell you they have the assurance that God's Holy Spirit dwells within them because Christ dwells within them. We look to the writings of the Apostle Paul who summarizes the entry of sin into the world and the hope of salvation.

Here are his words in the popular, Living Bible translation: "When Adam sinned, sin entered the entire human race. His sin spread death throughout all the world so everything began to grow old and die, for all sinned. We know that it was Adam's sin that caused this because although, of course, people were sinning from the time of Adam until Moses, God did not in those days judge them guilty of death for breaking his laws—because he had not yet given his laws to them nor told them what he wanted them to do. So when their bodies died it was not for their own sins since they themselves had never disobeyed God's special law against eating the forbidden fruit, as Adam had.

What a contrast between Adam and Christ who was yet to come! And what a difference between man's sin and God's forgiveness!

For this one man, Adam, brought death to many through his sin. But this one man, Jesus Christ, brought forgiveness to many through God's mercy. Adam's one sin brought the penalty of death to many, while Christ freely takes away many sins and gives glorious life instead.

The sin of this one man, Adam, caused death to be king over all, but all who will take God's gift of forgiveness and acquittal are kings of life because of this one man, Jesus Christ. Yes, Adam's sin brought punishment to all, but Christ's righteousness makes men right with God, so that they can live. Adam caused many to be sinners because he disobeyed God, and Christ caused many to be made acceptable to God because he obeyed."

THE FINAL SACRIFICE OFFERED TO GOD

The Ten Commandments were given so that people can see the extent of their failure to obey God's laws. But the more we recognize our sinfulness, the more we see God's abounding grace to forgive us. Before, sin ruled over all men and brought them to death; but now God's kindness rules instead, giving us right standing with God and resulting in eternal life through faith in Jesus Christ our Lord.

But before Jesus would come, coupled with the Ten Commandments was the necessity to find a way of gaining God's forgiveness when the laws were broken. For this purpose, God instituted the guidelines for a sacrificial offering. He established that without the shedding of blood there was no remission, no forgiveness for sin.

Under the law, the sacrifice the Jews were to offer Him had to be perfect - a Lamb without a spot or blemish. Jesus was the final and ultimate sacrifice presented to God. He was the flawless, sinless sacrifice. He fulfilled the law and the obligation God placed before man to be reconciled to Him. The letter to the Hebrews defines the transition from this kind of offering to the offering Jesus presented to God on the Cross:

"The old system of Jewish laws gave only a dim foretaste of the good things Christ would do for us. The sacrifices under the old system were repeated again and again, year after year, but even so they could never save those who lived under their rules." (Hebrews 10:1-LB)

The benefit of the death of Jesus on the cross, meant the end of the continuous sacrifice, the end of the search for redemption, and finally a restored relationship with God.

Like the continuous sacrifice of old, The Roman Catholic Mass seeks to duplicate again and again the crucifixion; placing on the individual the task of doing something to achieve God's saving grace and rejecting the idea of the finality of the crucifixion.

The Other Italians state, for them it was a "never-ending" vigil to attain forgiveness. Finally, they accepted the Biblical teaching that Jesus died once and for all!

St. Peter summed it up for all generations to understand: "He paid for you with the precious lifeblood of Christ, the sinless, spotless Lamb of God. God chose Him for this purpose long before the world began, but now in these final days, He was sent to the earth for all to see. And He did this for you." (1 Peter 1:19-20-LB)

Both Roman Catholics and The Other Italians recognize that someone had to pay the price to redeem mankind back to God. The rugged and splintered cross was mandatory in the plan of salvation for man, and God's grace was manifested on it once and for all.

Someone had to be the ultimate and final sacrifice presented to God as promised in the Garden of Eden. Man sinned, and it was only fair that he be the ultimate sacrifice for his sinful state! Yet, God chose His son Jesus to accomplish this on our behalf. The empty cross, nay the empty tomb, stands as a testimony to the finality of God's plan for mankind!

But here's the difference in beliefs. The Other Italians now embrace the Word of God rather than the ever evolving and changing words of man! As "spiritual," pious and "intelligent" as the words may sound, if they contradict the Bible they are discounted. Most important is that they accept the scriptures that state, He died "ONCE AND FOR ALL." In his Epistle, St. Peter wrote on the subject: "For Christ also hath once suffered for sins, the just for the unjust, that he might bring us to God, being put to death in the flesh, but quickened by the Spirit:" (St. Peter 3:18)

Archbishop Fulton J. Sheen is among the foremost theological scholars of the Roman Catholic Church, and wrote this for clarification regarding the purpose and significance of the MASS for Roman Catholics. If there is ever a question whether the Roman Catholic Mass conducts the "actual re-sacrifice of Christ on the cross," the following will serve as an affidavit of confirmation.

CALVARY AND THE MASS - A Missal Companion by Archbishop Fulton J. Sheen, Ph.D., D.D., LL.D., Litt.D.

The Church which Christ founded has not only preserved the Word He spoke, and the wonders He wrought; it has also taken Him seriously when He said: "Do this for a commemoration of me." And that action whereby we re-enact His Death on the Cross is the Sacrifice of the Mass, in which we do as a memorial what He did at the Last Supper as the pre-figuration of His Passion.

In "Eucharist Communion" we read the following:

"The Last Supper and the Holy Eucharist (the Mass) are both looking at Jesus' crucifixion from God's point of view. When you go into a Catholic church to attend Mass, what is happening on that altar is NOT a reenactment, not just a memorial, NOT just a representation, it IS the actual Sacrifice of Our Blessed Lord on the Cross." The message of Roman Catholic theologians has been consistent with the Canon of the Council of Trent (I, II, III - 1545-1563).

The Other Italians ask: Is the crucifixion to be repeated? Does Jesus die again and again in conflict with the scripture that says He died once and cannot die again? The Apostle Paul wrote a letter to the congregation in Rome. In it he makes a final deposition regarding the matter:

"Now if we have died with Christ, we believe that we shall also live with Him, knowing that Christ, having been raised from the dead, is never to die again; death no longer is master over Him. For the death that He died, He died to sin once for all but the life that He lives, He lives to God. Even so consider yourselves to be dead to sin, but alive to God in Christ Jesus." Romans 6:11)

One of the things The Other Italians related to this author was that in the past they were ignorant of the scriptures. When they were members of the Roman Catholic Church they were never encouraged to read the Bible, let alone be a lifetime student of it. Today, they believe all that one needs to know about God is written therein and revealed to them by the Holy Spirit.

They embrace the literal and factual text (The canon of Scriptures is accepted by both The Other Italians and The Roman Catholic Church) of the scriptures that the crucifixion, and death of Jesus on the cross was only needed one time. They believe His suffering and death does not have to be repeated again and again as with the sacrament of the Roman Catholic Mass! They accept the record found in the Bible in St. John 19:28, where just before his death Jesus uttered in an audible voice for all to hear:

"Tetelestai" means "IT IS FINISHED! No other sacrifice would ever be needed again

Chapter Eight:
Baptism

Coming from a Roman Catholic religious background, The Other Italians experienced the "sacrament" of Infant Baptism (a means of receiving God's grace according to RC doctrine). After they moved on to their new faith, they followed the "ordinance" of baptism as explained by St. Peter (A symbolic re-enactment of the life of Christ as described in the Gospels).

Factually, there is no record that St. Peter or any of the other Disciples ever baptized a baby; but we can conclude that they did indeed baptize those who confessed Jesus as Savior as recorded in the Gospels.

St. Peter explained the order of baptism when he said, "REPENT, and be baptized every one of you in the name of Jesus Christ…" (Acts 2:38)

Nowhere in the Bible is there evidence that God's saving grace is given on the basis of being sprinkled or immersed in a body of water. There is no theological argument for "baptismal regeneration." Arbitrary and erroneous interpretations of the Bible have caused great confusion with regards to this sacrament.

Throughout the New Testament there is an ordered pattern; the conscious act of repentance precedes baptism. This is the background of the scriptures dealing with the subject.

The Other Italians believe an individual must come to an age when he/she realizes that their sin separates them from God. Repentance follows; then baptism is in order to openly declare the desire to make Jesus the Lord of their lives.

The Other Italians now refer to Jesus as their "Lord;" not that they did not recognize the fact that Jesus is referred to as Lord in the sacraments and ceremonies but now the word has taken on a different meaning. For a moment, let's consider the meaning of the word and learn why there is a new significance to it in the life of the Born Again Christian!

First, the word Lord is used as a TITLE. The Bible message is quite dogmatic! There are two powers who wish to be master of a person's life: Jesus vs. Satan. Romans 6:14 says: "For sin shall not be master over you, for you are not under law but under grace." (Note the word, 'Master') Most individuals do not know that by virtue of choice (whether consciously or instinctively, he or she is already serving one of two masters who are vying for their life: Jesus and Satan). St Matthew makes the distinction: "No one can serve two masters; for either he will hate the one and love the other, or he will be devoted to one and despise the other." (Matthew 6:24) One will be the "Lord" of an individual's life!

It is also a NAME. In the Old Testament the name Lord is synonymous with these words, Jehovah, Yahweh, and Adonai. These designations for "God" were never spoken out loud by the Jews. Consider this scripture: "Being found in appearance as a man, He (Jesus) humbled Himself by becoming obedient to the point of death, even death on a cross. For this reason also, God highly exalted Him, and bestowed on Him the name which is above every name, so that at the name of Jesus every knee will bow, of those who are in heaven and on earth and under the earth, and that every tongue will confess that Jesus Christ is Lord, to the glory of God the Father." (1 Philippians 2:8-11)

Based on the scriptures, The Other Italians believe baptism is a time when an individual proclaims who is LORD of their life. The act of infant baptism may have cultural and religious roots but it has no saving power.

While we know the Disciples did not baptize babies, nowhere in the scriptures do we read of anyone else baptizing babies. The pattern is always "repent and be baptized." And while parents and grandparents can promise to raise the child in their faith, there is no substitutionary confession; that is they cannot repent on behalf of the child!

The Other Italians accept the Biblical premise that baptism is not a means of receiving or accepting God's grace. It serves as an affirmation - a sign to those about (family, friends, associates) that the person has made a life-changing decision to repent of their sins and accept God's grace through the death of His Son, Jesus. He alone becomes the Lord of their lives!

Proof of this pattern is found in the first chapter of the New Testament. There, in the Gospel according to St. John, we are introduced to a man, John (not the author) who is preaching a message to his audience that they had to repent and get ready for the appearance of the Messiah. To acknowledge their repentance and faith, he baptized them. It was not the emersion into the Jordon River that saved them, but their open confession of faith. This is the first recorded incidence in the New Testament where we find people being baptized by 'submersion.'

In this initial record we observe people accepting the message of salvation by faith alone. Like those who John baptized, The Other Italians were baptized after they believed. This issue remains an "irreconcilable difference."

The Other Italians have now been baptized by immersion; that is to be actually submerged down under the water. The message of the Bible indicates that this 'ordinance' depicts the individual dying to sin, being buried and coming forth to new life in Christ. Baptism by immersion is symbolic! It is an outward expression of the inward change one has experienced having been regenerated by the Spirit of God. Again, it is a public demonstration where the individual "testifies" of his/her faith in Christ before family, friends and the church. The Other Italians believe in baptism by submersion as described in the scriptures. In all cases, only God can judge the intent of the man or woman who is being babtized.

The New Testament was first written in Greek, and the word baptism (Baptizo) means to "to submerge" - "to go down under."

Every account in the New Testament where someone is baptized has the individual "going down into the waters." There is no sprinkling or any other means of baptism described. As an example, Jesus humbled himself and confirmed John's ministry and baptism by submersion.

In the book of Acts, Saint Paul presents a summation of John's baptism: "Then said Paul, John verily baptized with the baptism of repentance, saying unto the people, that they should believe on him which should come after him, that is, on Christ Jesus." Acts 19:4

Here is that same scripture as found in the Living Bible: "Then Paul pointed out to them that John's baptism was to demonstrate a desire to turn from sin to God and that those receiving his baptism must then go on to believe in Jesus, the one John said would come later."

John preached a new message to the people…it pointed the way of salvation through ONE who would come after him…the promised Messiah. Note, the personal confession of sins by an individual was an entirely new idea to the children of Israel…his listeners. For the Israelite the "Day of Atonement" was a time when the sins of the whole nation were brought before the Lord God. Now, with the advent of the promised messiah…they would have a direct and personal relationship with God.

Those who responded to John's message of repentance exhibited a personal act of contrition by going down into the waters. The waters did not save them - their faith did! Thus, they turned from their historic religion and placed their faith, not in a new religion, but in Jesus the Christ! Those who believed and accepted this message at that time testified to those about with the action of baptism in the Jordon River.

The Other Italians understand that baptism is not a means of salvation, that is to believe, you receive God's grace by the submitting to the action. They rely on the testimony of the Holy Scriptures which warn there is nothing man can do to inherit God's forgiveness: "For by grace you have been saved through faith; and that not of yourselves, it is the gift of God; not as a result of works, so that no one may boast." (Ephesians 2:8-9)

Nowhere in the scriptures does it say or imply: "By baptism you are saved!" The Other Italians understand that they can do nothing to receive the saving grace of God. They trust it is achieved only through faith in Jesus and accepting Him as their own personal LORD and SAVIOR. They recognize Jesus' death on the cross as a final sacrifice offered to God. Baptism by immersion tells their friends, family and associates of this decision.

Chapter Nine: Transubstantiation

Transubstantiation is the belief that during a Mass, the bread and wine actually become the body and blood of Jesus. This is the heart of Roman Catholicism!

Interestingly, I interviewed one hundred young people who were in and around the age of eighteen and members of the Church. Only seven stated that the bread and wine actually became the body and blood of Jesus. Of the over one hundred adults (21-75) interviewed, only seventeen stated it actually became the body and blood of Jesus.

It is by no means a "scientific" study, but it does give some insight into the behavioral trends within the Church.

According to the Roman Catholic Canon, the appearance of the bread and wine does not change its physical form; but it does become the actual presence of Jesus. Because they are believed to be the very presence of Christ Himself - Church members worship and adore the elements.

The Other Italians reject this mystical "transformation" (Transubstantiation) because they hold to the scripture that proclaims Christ died once and for all. The repetition of the crucifixion or symbolic crucifixion through the Mass is rejected. Their reasons: St. Peter himself gives the answer in his writings "For Christ also hath once suffered for sins, the just for the unjust, that he might bring us to God, being put to death in the flesh, but quickened by the Spirit:" (1 Peter 3:18)

The teaching of the Church is that the Mass is a "bloodless" crucifixion. In this sacrament, Jesus offers His blood again and again. There is no "ceremonial crucifixion" or re-enactment recorded anywhere in the Bible commemorating the actual death of Jesus Christ.

Throughout the Old Testament the Children of Israel had to offer a blood sacrifice as per the requirements of the Law. The death of Jesus was foretold throughout the Old Testament and the writers describe it in vivid detail. In His death, the final and ultimate blood offering was presented to God. It would be for the propitiation of our sins. That's an unfamiliar word to most, but in essence we would win God's favor by the sacrificial death of Jesus! St John 1:7 wrote: "But if we walk in the light, as He is in the light, we have fellowship one with another, and the blood of Jesus Christ His Son cleanseth us from all sin." (St. John 1:7)

At the ecumenical assembly of the Roman Catholic Church, known as the: The Council of Trent (1545-63) the following was issued with regards to the MASS. The Council declared – "The same Christ who offered himself once in a bloody manner on the altar of the cross, is present and offered in an un-bloody manner."

The Other Italians site the scripture that says: "Without the shedding of blood there is no remission of sins!" (Hebrews 9:2). Based on the scriptures, they reject an "un-bloody" sacrifice.

The Other Italians rely on the full context of the scriptures and the account of the supper where the Lord Himself established the "Holy Communion." They acknowledge a very important time-line issue in this matter. Jesus himself said: "DO THIS IN REMEMBRANCE OF ME!"

Now consider this: He had not yet gone to the cross, which would have made this a "before the fact" occurrence. Until He would die on the cross…no blood was spilled!

Throughout the New Testament the message of the communion is one of looking back and "remembering."

In a letter to the Church in Corinth the Apostle Paul wrote this: "For as often as you eat this bread and drink this cup, you proclaim the Lord's death until he comes." (1 Corinthians 11:26) (Proclaim: To announce publically, declare, state, make known, to tell about). The scriptures clarify the meaning of the verse as a "broadcast, assertion or decree." The communion ceremony is a testimony to the world that Jesus not only died but he also came forth from the grave.

The Other Italians believe the bread and wine remain symbols of the death of Jesus. Further, they hold to some fundamental ideas concerning the "Table of the Lord."

- Nowhere in the entire Bible is the idea that Jesus' actual body and blood can be found in any earthly element. Jesus often spoke in spiritual terms throughout His ministry. This confounded people...especially religious leaders. The Disciple John wrote: "It is the Spirit who gives life; the flesh profits nothing; the words that I have spoken to you are spirit and are life." John 6:63 "The Spirit gives life!" These kinds of expressions surely confused the Jewish religious leaders of the day because the dutiful and pious religious matters were always dealt in concrete, physical, and especially legal terms.

- Jesus spoke "symbolically" when he was talking about eating his flesh and drinking his blood. The idea that an earthly element (bread and wine) actually transforms into the blood and body of Jesus is not supported literally or contextually in the many scriptures relating to His life, death, resurrection and second-coming. The idea of a "miraculous transformation" of the bread and wine appears nowhere in the scriptures.

- After that first communion the elements were referred to as "bread" and "wine." In St Matthew's gospel Jesus looks at his disciples and says: "This is my blood - but I say to you, I will not drink of this fruit of the vine from now on until that day when I drink it new with you in My Father's kingdom," (Matthew 26:29). Why would Jesus speak figuratively of His blood as "the fruit of the vine" if He meant it to be his literal blood? Would He not have called it that? Jesus called it "wine!"

- After the full institution of the communion supper was established in the New Testament Church...the elements were always referred to as wine and bread. The Apostle Saint Paul further establishes the communion with the early church in his letter to the Corinthians. "For as often as you eat this bread and drink the cup, you proclaim the Lord's death until He comes. Therefore whoever eats the bread or drinks the cup of the Lord in an unworthy manner, shall be guilty of the body and the blood of the Lord. But let a man examine himself, and so let him eat of the bread and drink of the cup..." I Corinthians 11:26-38)

If the elements were changed and were really bread and wine, then why does Paul refer to the bread as bread, and not the literal body of Jesus Christ?

- The disciples were not shocked or even surprised at Jesus' statements regarding "My Blood, "My Body?" There is no reaction on their part. There is no indication that they believed it was anything more than symbols because they had come accustomed to the metaphors and other figures of speech they lived with on a daily basis with Jesus.

- The Other Italians reason that if the bread was really the body and wine the blood, then Jesus would also be many other things (Literally) that he spoke of in his sermons when He said I am: a vine, a door, a gate, a light, bread. There is no indication in the entire Bible...the writings of the Disciples, Apostles and others that the "elements" were ever worshipped.

- The Holy Supper, as we have come to call it, where Jesus ate the Passover meal with his Disciples took place before Jesus went to the cross.

- The question remains: How could the wine and bread on the table be turned into something based on an event that had not occurred?

- Jesus is the only person who ever lived a sinless life...never violating the laws of God. He was a Jew and it would have been a violation of Jewish law to drink blood. If the wine actually became his blood, and he drank it, He would have not been sinless. (Leviticus 17:10)

> For Jesus to be the spotless Lamb of God He had to be sinless. Under the law there were grave consequences for one who shed and ate blood.

- The Other Italians lean on the scriptures for clarification regarding this matter. The Crucifixion of Jesus was prophesied to be a one-time offering…the final sacrifice to be offered to God for the forgiveness of sin. Consider the letter written by the Apostle Paul: "By this will we have been sanctified through the offering of the body of Jesus Christ once for all. And every priest stands daily ministering and offering time after time the same sacrifices, which can never take away sins; but He, having offered one sacrifice for sins for all time, sat down at the right hand of God, waiting from that time onward until His enemies be made a footstool for His feet. For by one offering He has perfected for all time those who are sanctified." (Hebrews 10:14)

- The act of eating and drinking, whether one believes it is the actual body and blood of Jesus for the purpose of receiving God's grace, places on the individual the obligation to do something to receive it. Salvation for mankind is based on the premise that there is nothing that can be done to earn it! It is God's ultimate GIFT to mankind.

So, The Other Italians reject the idea that they have to do anything to receive God's grace and blessing. The scriptures define this further."…being justified as a gift by His grace through the redemption which is in Christ Jesus," (Romans 3:24). God's forgiving grace is a free gift; it goes beyond what one might expect and it is a gift that is given freely!

"Therefore we conclude that a man is justified by faith without the deeds of the law," (Romans. 3:28). Mankind can do nothing to earn it or achieve it! "For what saith the scripture? Abraham believed God, and it was counted unto him for righteousness," (Romans 4:3). There is no record or implication in the scriptures that a person ever received the gift of salvation by doing something.

There is a chapter in the Bible that declares the men and women of old were counted as "righteous" as a result of their trust and faith in God alone.

"For the promise to Abraham or to his descendants that he would be heir of the world was not through the Law, but through the righteousness of faith," (Romans 4:13).

"Therefore being justified by faith, we have peace with God through our Lord Jesus Christ," (Romans 5:1).

The Other Italians accept as true that we can do nothing to achieve a relationship with God outside of a relationship with His son, Jesus. Consider the clarity of Romans 10:8-10: "But what saith it? The word is nigh thee, even in thy mouth, and in thy heart: that is, the word of faith, which we preach;" That if thou shalt confess with thy mouth the Lord Jesus, and shalt believe in thine heart that God hath raised him from the dead, thou shalt be saved. For with the heart man believeth unto righteousness; and with the mouth confession is made unto salvation."

Here is that same scripture as presented in the Living Bible: For salvation that comes from trusting Christ—which is what we preach—is already within easy reach of each of us; in fact, it is as near as our own hearts and mouths. For if you tell others with your own mouth that Jesus Christ is your Lord and believe in your own heart that God has raised him from the dead, you will be saved. For it is by believing in his heart that a man becomes right with God; and with his mouth he tells others of his faith, confirming his salvation.

Sounds simple and it is; so simple people have to battle within themselves to accept the gift of salvation! The argument within the mind of people is that there must be something he or she can do to merit God's love and forgiveness. "It just can't be free!" Yet, it is fully documented in St. Paul's letter to the Ephesians: "For by grace you have been saved through faith; and that not of yourselves, IT IS THE GIFT OF GOD; not as a result of works, so that no one may boast." (Ephesians 2:8-9)

The Other Italians reject the "religiosity" (the piety, rituals, obedience and servitude of religion), and have accepted God's gift. The message of the Old and New Testaments is that there was to be a single sacrifice for the sin of mankind. It was proclaimed in the Garden of Eden, runs through the books of the Bible, leading to the crucifixion and resurrection. The message is, "Once and for all!"

Chapter Ten:
Saints and Sainthood

The idea of proclaiming individuals as "Saints" in the Roman Catholic Church began sometime during the tenth century, and originally centered on Martyrs who served the early Church. The path leading to Sainthood is a significant historic and traditional journey. The worship and reverence of Saints has evolved over the centuries and today is very much a part of Roman Catholic worship. Parishioners are taught that Saints serve as "intercessors" for them, and are acknowledged with special Masses and celebrations.

For one to become a "Saint," it must be proven that he or she lived a righteous life - having exercised a constant faith and dedication to the Church. There are also stages or levels leading to sainthood: SERVANT OF GOD, VENERABLE, BLESSED. The Other Italians no longer accept the elevation of spiritual status with individuals here on earth or in the hereafter. Again, they trust only the scriptures that do not record the use of the word "SAINT" as a superior state within the Body of Christ.

The New Testament indicates that Peter, Paul and the other Apostles greeted the members of the local congregations as "Saints." It was used to identify "believers" much the same as calling someone "brother" or "sister" which is more commonly used in the local churches where The Other Italians attend.

In the religious sense, Sainthood is bestowed on one who was confirmed as being "Holy." The Other Italians declare their identity as, "sinners saved by grace;" and while there are individuals who are involved in good works, ministry, and dedicated service, they achieve no greater station here or in heaven.

But why do Roman Catholics believe in granting "Sainthood" for individuals? As stated, their Church believes people who are given Sainthood can provide another means of reaching God on their behalf. The parishioner can pray to a Saint, who in turn, prays for them in heaven – petitioning God on their behalf. This is called "Beatific Vision." This dogma is totally rejected by The Other Italians who site the words of Jesus in their response: "I am the way, and the truth, and the life; no one comes to the Father, but through me." (John 14:6)

"I told you that you would die in your sins; if you do not believe that I am the one I claim to be, you will indeed die in your sins." (John 8:24)

St. Paul also declares the sovereignty or dominion of Jesus. "Salvation is found in no one else, for there is no other name under heaven given to men by which we must be saved." (Acts 4:12) "For there is one God and one mediator between God and men, the man Christ Jesus!" (1 Timothy 2:5)

The Other Italians explain it thus: "What Jesus did on the cross was to provide "the way" (not, "a way") to God by being the final sacrifice for the sins of mankind. Only He is Holy - right from the foundation of the earth…and does not need to be venerated. The Bible says He is above all! When we pray, it is Jesus who goes to the Father and intercedes just like the Bible says!" In St. Paul's Letter to the Saints in Philippi (Philippians 2:5-11) he writes: "Let this mind be in you, which was also in Christ Jesus, who, being in the form of God, did not consider it robbery to be equal with God, but made Himself of no reputation, taking the form of a bondservant, and coming in the likeness of men. And being found in appearance as a man, He humbled Himself and became obedient to the point of death, even the death of the cross. Therefore God also has highly exalted Him and given Him the name which is above every name that at the name of Jesus every knee should bow, of those in heaven, and of those on earth, and of those under the earth and that every tongue should confess that Jesus Christ is Lord, to the glory of God the Father."

The Lord Jesus cannot be duplicated, copied, emulated, and in no way does He need mankind to elevate Him by any means they may think is spiritual or "religious." He is the Holy Son of the Almighty.

Another interesting fact is that the word "saint" is also used in the Old Testament to identify believers or members of the congregation:

"O love the LORD, all ye his saints: for the LORD preserveth the faithful, and plentifully rewardeth (in the sense of punishment) the proud doer." (Psalms 31:23)

Throughout the scriptures there seems to be a singular definition for the word "Saint." Individuals who are referred to as such are those that are recognized as being "set apart." Surrendering your will to Christ sets you apart from the past and those who outright reject Jesus. The idea of being set apart is consistent with the scriptures that recognize the spiritual state of that person. Such are called, by the New Testament Apostles - "SAINTS!

The Other Italians (Bible believing Christians) believe all regenerated Christians are Saints but fully understand this does not mean they walk around with a halo around their head (Hollywood depiction) As stated, the Apostle St. Paul used the salutation "Saints" when he wrote his letters and there was a reason why he did so! He called them "Saints" so to indicate he was addressing the "sanctified" members of a society…those who were set apart! The early New Testament believer was fully aware that the salutation was an identification of their citizenship in a unique spiritual body of individuals, and not that they had any divine superiority. The Other Italians do revere and respect many who have served mankind, but the idea of elevating their spiritual status does not have a Biblical foundation.

Chapter Eleven:
Rosary and Rituals

Many of the rituals of the Roman Catholic Church evolved during the period 12th to the 15th centuries; one of which was the ritual of praying the Rosary. We have come to call this period the "Middle Ages" (1050 – 1450). To fully understand why The Other Italians do not pray the Rosary or participate in the historic rituals one must look into the origins of these practices.

The Twentieth Century Encyclopedia of Catholicism contains the following regarding the foundation for its beliefs:

"The missionary history of the [Catholic] Church clearly shows her adaptability to all races, all continents, all nations. In her liturgy and her art, in her tradition and the forming of her doctrine, naturally enough she includes Jewish elements, but also elements that are of pagan origin. In certain respects, she has copied her organization from that of the Roman Empire, has preserved and made fruitful the philosophical intuitions of Socrates, Plato and Aristotle, borrowed from both Barbarians and the Byzantine Roman Empire—but always remains herself, thoroughly digesting all elements drawn from external sources...In her laws, her ceremonies, her festivals and her devotions, she makes use of local customs after purifying them and baptizing them."

The Other Italians reject the practice of adopting customs and practices from various cultures and making them a part of their worship. Nowhere in the scriptures are pagan and barbarian rituals "sanctified" by an act of baptism. They contend that it is not in the nature of Holy God, to purify local customs, especially those of "satanic origin" to accommodate one group of people or another. They believe evangelism must be based on the practices found in the scriptures, and not on the adaptation or imitation of customs and traditions. As for assimilating pagan practices in worship, and accepting "external sources"- rather than the Holy Bible, they consider this nothing less than blasphemous!

The Roman Catholic Church has evolved over the centuries with dogma that has been adopted to preserve its ecclesiastical integrity. The centuries testify to its doctrinal evolution. The Other Italians accept the immutable (unassailable) scriptures as their final authority.

This timeline shows the adoption of certain beliefs

Doctrine	Date
Relic Worship	337 Ad
Rosary	366ad
Mass	394 Ad
Eternal Torment	590 Ad
Indulgences	799 Ad
Mary Worship	850 Ad
Confessional	1198 Ad
Bible Reading Forbidden	1299 Ad
Infant Baptism	1311 Ad
Tradition Above Scripture	1563 Ad

The Other Italians reject the ever-evolving religious practices and requirements of their former church. Their objections are again based on what they call the truths of the Bible. For example, in its history, the Roman Catholic Church has offered INDULGENCES (leniency and forgiveness for sin) to its members in exchange for favors or monetary endowments. Today, the Church has re-defined the meaning of indulgences as "extra sacramental remission," and the Catholic Encyclopedia states this: "...the

Church has received from Christ the power to grant indulgences..." Nowhere in the Bible is there any direct or indirect reference to "extra sacramental remission of sins" other than by the one time sacrifice of the blood of Jesus).

The encyclopedia continues: "...In theological language also the word is sometimes employed in its primary sense to signify the kindness and mercy of God. But in the special sense in which it is here considered, an indulgence is a remission of the temporal punishment due to sin, the guilt of which has been forgiven."

In response to this The Other Italians reference the words of the Lord as found in Matthew 28:18: "And Jesus came and spake unto them, saying, all power is given unto me in heaven and in earth."

St. John wrote:

"But if we walk in the light, as he is in the light, we have fellowship one with another, and the blood of Jesus Christ his Son cleanseth us from all sin." 1 John 1:7

The Other Italians hold to the scripture that indicate only by the "blood of Jesus is there forgiveness of sins." This is also reiterated in Paul's letter to the Romans: "Much more then, being now justified by his blood, we shall be saved from wrath through him." (Romans 5:9)

THE ROSARY

Among the most cherished practices of the Roman Catholic Church is praying the ROSARY. The Other Italians recognize the fact that there is no mention of praying the Rosary in the Bible; nor is there any system or incantation presented therein; and nowhere in the Bible is Mary named, called or crowned the "Queen of Heaven."

The Rosary centers on Mary, and her assumed position in relation to Jesus and God the Father. According to the Rosary prayer, Mary is an advocate with the Father ("Mary our precious advocate"), an intermediary between man and God, devotion ("our life and our hope")-("Holy").

A question arises when we believe anyone to be "Holy" and can serve as a substitute for Christ. If God is Holy, what man or woman could be the same? Who can remove sins? "HOLY" is a descriptor reserved only for God. Further, Colossian 1:27 speaks of mankind's hope for salvation: "to whom God willed to make known what is the riches of the glory of this mystery among the Gentiles, which is Christ in you, the hope of glory."

The Other Italians believe the scriptures that promise, Jesus is our hope!

WAS MARY SINLESS?

Down through history many attributes have been given to the person of Jesus' mother. But a careful examination of the Scriptures will find that it is Mary who clarifies who she is in God's plan for her life. Her famous, and often quoted prayer, The Magnificat, is most revealing and cannot be discounted in the discussion of her being "deity." If she is deity, she must be sinless! If she was sinless, why did she pray at the time of the annunciation: "my soul doth magnify the Lord, and my spirit hath rejoiced in God my Savior?" (Luke 1:46-47) People who are sinners need a Savior!

The Church teaches that an individual prays the Rosary to be reminded of the mysteries of salvation and to receive the promises of God ("Grace for the forgiveness of sins") through the Blessed Mother.

The Other Italians believe the only way to God is through Jesus: "For God sent not His Son into the world to condemn the world, but that the WORLD through Him might be SAVED." (John 3:17)

The message of the scriptures is always, "through Him, and "by Him." The Bible does not contain one word that speaks of anyone "facilitating" the plan of redemption other than the Son of God, Jesus the Christ!

The Other Italians accept the scriptures that state only Jesus can save us from sin, and is the only intermediary before God the Father. They ask; "who is the man or woman or religious institution that can add or take away form the truths of the scriptures and by what authority?"

As for praying the Rosary, they again site the scriptures that clarify the issue of prayer to God. It is the Lord's Disciple, Matthew who documented the account where Jesus was teaching His audience about prayer: "But thou, when thou prayest, enter into thy closet, and when thou hast shut thy door, pray to thy Father which is in secret; and thy Father which seeth in secret shall reward thee openly. But when ye pray, use not vain repetitions, as the heathen do: for they think that they shall be heard for their much speaking." (Matt 6:6-7)

Jesus rebuked the words and practices off ceremonial prayer. Here is another look at this scripture in the Living Bible: "Don't recite the same prayer over and over as the heathen do, who think prayers are answered only by repeating them again and again. Remember, your Father knows exactly what you need even before you ask him!"

Repetitious prayers are those that are routine, as in chanting a series of words over and over again, praying a certain way or with certain words at specific times of the day. Jesus was obviously familiar with pagan religions of His day, and did not want believers to pray as they prayed. Their belief was that by repeating prayers over and over again, they would be answered.

It is by definition, ritualistic prayer, and beads of any kind support repetitious prayers.

The Other Italians have learned that many of the traditions, customs and accepted rituals of the Roman Catholic Church are rooted in exactly that…the customs, traditions of people and rituals of other cultures and religions. And because these are not found in the Bible, they are subject to the many arguments of theologians and scholars who question their exact historical roots, and reasons for adoption by the Roman Catholic Church in their worship.

For instance, the Church adopted the practice of praying the Rosary from St. Dominic (Circa 1221) when he claimed to have received a vision of the Blessed Mother.

But Catholic scholars like English Priest Fr. Henry Charles Thurston (1856-1939) who is a prolific scholar on liturgical, literary, historical, and spiritual matters argues the legitimacy of the "appearance" to St. Dominic because, he believed, "it lacked an historical foundation." Other scholars document the use of prayer beads prior to his alleged apparitional claim.

Yet, stories of Dominic's vision continued through the years by means of oral tradition, and were further supported by Alan de la Roche, a Priest

(1428-1475). His own credibility, in the matter of St Dominic's vision, has been historically "questioned."

Thurston wrote over one hundred and fifty articles for the Catholic Encyclopedia; one of which states: "Alan was a very earnest and devout man, but, as the highest authorities admit, he was full of delusions, and based his revelations on the imaginary testimony of writers that never existed…" Thurston also asserted, "Alan bases his claim on the above-mentioned "imaginary" writers and on private revelations."

Unsubstantiated and questionable oral traditions, un-assuredness, and debate, account for some of the reasons why The Other Italians have embraced the Bible as their source of truth. St. Paul warned the church in Colossae about adopting the "traditions" and practices of man: "See to it that no one takes you captive through philosophy and empty deception, according to the tradition of men, according to the elementary principles of the world, rather than according to Christ."

His message was tri-fold: First - totally reject pagan practices; Second - cease your obedience man-made religious creeds; Third - scrutinize and rebuff any false teaching that contradicts the Word of God

The Other Italians embrace the promise of Jesus who said: "…when He, the Spirit of truth, is come, He will guide you into all truth:"

Again, the idea or doctrine of praying the Rosary appears nowhere in the Scriptures. The only reference that can be incurred comes from Jesus who warned against praying repetitiously found in Matthew 6:7: "But when ye pray, use not vain repetitions!" Here's the extended verse from the Living Bible: "When you pray, don't babble on and on as people of other religions do. They think their prayers are answered merely by repeating their words again and again."

Perhaps one can learn the mind of Jesus by reading one of His final prayers: There are no repetitions, no chants, and no formulas - just heart to heart communication.

"After Jesus said this, he looked toward heaven and prayed: "Father, the time has come. Glorify your Son, that your Son may glorify you. For you granted him authority over all people that he might give eternal life to all those you have given him. Now this is eternal life: that they may know you, the only true God, and Jesus Christ, whom you have sent. I have brought you glory on earth by completing the work you gave me to do. And now, Father, glorify me in your presence with the glory I had with you before the world began. "I have revealed you to those whom you gave me out of the world. They were yours; you gave them to me and they have obeyed your word. Now they know that everything you have given me comes from you. For I gave them the words you gave me and they accepted them. They knew with certainty that I came from you, and they believed that you sent me. I pray for them. I am not praying for the world, but for those you have given me, for they are yours. All I have is yours, and all you have is mine. And glory has come to me through them. I will remain in the world no longer, but they are still in the world, and I am coming to you. Holy Father, protect them by the power of your name--the name you gave me--so that they may be one as we are one. While I was with them, I protected them and kept them safe by that name you gave me. None has been lost except the one doomed to destruction so that Scripture would be fulfilled. "I am coming to you now, but I say these things while I am still in the world, so that they may have the full measure of my joy within them. I have given them your word and the world has hated them, for they are not of the world any more than I am of the world. My prayer is not that you take them out of the world but that you protect them from the evil one. They are not of the world, even as I am not of it. Sanctify them by the truth; your word is truth. As you sent me into the world, I have sent them into the world. For them I sanctify myself, that they too may be truly sanctified. "My prayer is not for them alone. I pray also for those who will believe in me through their message, that all of them may be one, Father, just as you are in me and I am in you. May they also be in us so that the world may believe that you have sent me. I have given them the glory that you gave me, that they may be one as we are one: I in them and you in me. May they be brought to complete unity to let the world know that you sent me and have loved them even as you have loved me. "Father, I want those you have given me to be with me where I am, and to see my glory, the glory you have given me because you loved me before the creation of the world. "Righteous Father, though the world does not know you, I know you, and they know that you have sent me. I have made you known to them, and will continue to make you known in order that the love you have for me may be in them and that I myself may be in them." (St. John 17:1-26)

Chapter Twelve:
The Lord's Prayer

The LORD'S PRAYER has become a significant part of liturgy in most Christian Churches. The Other Italians also pray it; but with an understanding of its merit and purpose that is quite different than Roman Catholics.

Jesus prayed, what is known as, The Lord's Prayer, in response to a question posed by one of His Disciples. St Matthew records the event in chapter 6:9-13. He requested, "Lord, teach us to pray!"

Jesus answered: "This, then, is how you should pray!" Keep in mind the Disciple did not ask Jesus for a specific prayer; he asks for instruction on how, not what to pray. Prayer was a historically a very ritualistic activity. Jesus understood this and did not answer the question by rendering a "fixed" prayer or prayers. This was the pattern of "religious," and pagan prayer; so one doesn't have to wonder why the Disciple asked the question in the way he did. Jesus answers the request by saying - "this is HOW" you should pray. He did not say this is what or when you should say. Again, religious and pagan prayer included beads, ordered prayers, and times to recite them. He spoke this:

"Our Father who is in heaven, hallowed be Your name.
Your kingdom come Your will be done on earth as it is in heaven.
Give us this day our daily bread.

And forgive us our debts, as we also have forgiven our debtors.
And do not lead us into temptation, but deliver us from evil.
For Yours is the kingdom and the power and the glory forever."

Jesus gave us less than seventy words and presented a perfect <u>pattern</u> for prayer. The Other Italians do not believe there is any spiritual power or superiority in the prayer. They see it as a reverent guide to approach the Almighty. Some theologians cite the prayer as a "skeleton" - a foundation for our own personal words and thoughts. In another sense one can see specific meaning to each phrase as presented here.

The noted minister, Rev. Dr. John MacArthur has rendered an understandable guide to this portion of scripture:

"When outlined from the perspective of our relationship to God, we see: Our Father showing the father/child relationship; hallowed be Thy name, the deity/worshiper; Thy kingdom come, the sovereign/subject; Thy will be done, the master/servant; give us this day our daily bread, the benefactor/beneficiary; forgive us our debts, the Savior/sinner; and do not lead us into temptation, the guide/pilgrim.

From the perspective of the attitude and spirit of prayer, <u>Our</u> reflects unselfishness; <u>Father</u> reflects family devotion; <u>hallowed be Thy name</u>, reverence; <u>Thy kingdom come</u>, loyalty; <u>Thy will be done</u>, submission; <u>give us this day our daily bread</u>, dependence; <u>forgive us our debts,</u> penitence; <u>do not lead us into temptation</u>, humility; <u>Thine is the kingdom</u>, triumph; <u>and the glory</u>, exultation; <u>and forever</u>, hope.

In similar ways the prayer can be outlined to show (1) the balance of God's glory and our need; (2) the threefold purpose of prayer: to hallow God's name, bring in His kingdom, and do His will; and (3) the approach of present (give us this day our daily bread), past (forgive us our debts), and future (do not lead us into temptation). (Taken from the GRACE TO YOU- John MacArthur-www.gtv.org)"

An individual or group can certainly pray this magnificent prayer but The Other Italians recognize something that is significant. Nowhere in the entire New Testament does Peter, Paul or any New Testament writer ever pray, refer to or use the prayer again.

So let's look at the scriptural context of this prayer. The Lord utters this prayer in answer to a question: "Lord, HOW should we pray?" He doesn't go into the prayer immediately. He prefaces his remarks with a general explanation as to how people were praying at the time. Most religions had repetitive incantations and chant-like prayers that were created by religious founders and leaders.

One must keep in mind that at this time the masses were uneducated, perhaps "a-literate," in the sense that they knew the language for essential communication purposes; and some could write it sparingly. Communication was simple and basic. Heretofore, prayers were learned and repeated. Jesus' prayer called for personal and intimate communication with God. On that day, Jesus was changing all of the "rules" set forth by religion! Now it would be spontaneous and personal!

If we back up to the first verses in this chapter we see the context of Jesus' message: "When you pray, you are not to be like the hypocrites; for they love to stand and pray in the synagogues and on the street corners so that they may be seen by men. Truly I say to you, they have their reward in full. But you, when you pray, go into your inner room, close your door and pray to your Father who is in secret, and your Father who sees what is done in secret will reward you. And when you are praying, do not use meaningless repetition as the Gentiles do, for they suppose that they will be heard for their many words. So do not be like them; for your Father knows what you need before you ask Him."

The prayer, as model, gives the prayer an understanding of the nature of God and his or her relationship to Him.

Jesus points out that prayer is a humble thing

While there are many interpretations as to the reason why Jesus prayed this prayer a critique of the verses above is important. He instructs his audience with these words. (Matthew 6:6) But thou, when thou prayest, enter into thy closet, and when thou hast shut thy door, pray to thy Father which is in secret; and thy Father which seeth in secret shall reward thee openly.

Jesus teaches that prayer is a personal thing. And there is a reward for this humility.

But when ye pray, use not vain repetitions, as the heathen do: for they think that they shall be heard for their much speaking. Be not ye therefore like unto them: for your Father knoweth what things ye have need of, before ye ask him.

Jesus tells His audience God already knows what is in your heart and mind.

As already written above, He offers a PATTERN (or skeleton) for prayer. If we prayed this over and over again…it would be "vain repetition." No matter how many times we pray it…there is no power in it!

"After this manner, therefore pray ye: Our Father which art in heaven, Hallowed be thy name."

Jesus subjected Himself to the "will of His Father in heaven and tells His audience they must be subject to His will as well!

"Thy kingdom come, Thy will be done in earth, as it is in heaven."

Jesus states prayer is an unselfish act as God has already promised to provide for our needs.

"Give us this day our daily bread."

Jesus tells his audience that only God can forgive our sins (debts) and we must forgive those who sin against us.

"And forgive us our debts, as we forgive our debtors."

Jesus gives a quick theological lesson to His audience.

Satan is the author of sin. He is the tempter. The prayer here is that God would protect them from the powers of Satan to draw them into sinful situations.

"And lead us not into temptation, but deliver us from evil:"

Jesus dealt heavily with the religious instincts of mankind.

He holds the all-inclusive power over the Christian's life. No other person or institution can claim even a piece of God's power and sovereignty.

"For thine is the kingdom, and the power, and the glory, forever. Amen."

The Other Italians follow the pattern by addressing God the Father in the name of Jesus. (Jesus said: "No man comes to the Father but by me" – St. John 14:6)

Final thoughts: The prayer Jesus gave was not meant to be repeated as a prayer in and of itself. This is clear for several reasons. Jesus says when you pray, "PRAY, THEN IN THIS WAY." (The word He uses is HOUTOS OUN (Greek) - which interpreted means, "then, in this way.") Jesus answered the disciple's question in a matter of fact fashion to teach the individual how to approach God in prayer.

For The Other Italians, the Lord's Prayer is a guide for prayer. They do not recite rote prayers or prayers for special occasions and celebrations. They address God the Father and they pray, exclusively, in the Name of Jesus.

Chapter Thirteen:
Genuflection

The act of bowing (lowering oneself on one or two knees or bending knees) before a superior dates back to the earliest times as an action showing respect for a person of honor and station. Alexander the Great instituted the custom in 328 BC. It was probably adopted from the courts in Middle East (Persia) and carried over into the Middle Ages. In recent years the ceremonial custom found the young man bowing before his intended and presenting a ring as a symbol of love and devotion.

In many religions bowing or kneeling is very much a part of worship protocol. Seen as a humbling and yielding, the individual symbolically prostrates him/herself in honor and admiration.

As early as the 1500s the Roman Catholic Church officially adopted the practice. Members are required to bow before a church altar and the Communion table. Today, the individual follows a full protocol for genuflecting in church before the sacraments.

Making the sign of the cross is a prayer in and of itself, and the belief is that God is at the altar; therefore the individual must acknowledge Him with this kind of reverence. The act of genuflecting is completely formalized in Roman Catholic worship. There are nine points during the Eucharist ceremony when the individual is expected to make the sign of cross:

1. The individual will make the sign of the cross: In the name of the Father, and of the Son, and of the Holy Ghost, Amen
2. At the words of Absolution or forgiveness of sins, after the General Confession
3. At the beginning of the Gospel reading
4. At the end of the prayer for the dead in the intercession
5. (During the Prayer of Consecration) When the Consecrated Host is raised
6. When the Chalice is raised
7. At Holy Communion before receiving the Host
8. Before receiving the Chalice
9. When the priest pronounces the final blessing

The Other Italians do not genuflect because the scriptures say that God dwells within the individual not at an altar or any given place where one might think or be told, He is present.

We've already learned that in the Old Testament the Jews were instructed to build a temple and God would dwell therein behind a veil. It was known as the Holy of Holies; no one could enter the Holy of Holies but the High Priest.

A veil in the temple separated man from God because the "final" sacrifice had not yet been offered. Mankind could not enter the presence of God until there was reconciliation. That came through the death of Jesus Christ.

Here is the scripture that testifies to this event:

'Jesus, when he had cried again with a loud voice, yielded up the ghost. And, behold, the veil of the temple was rent in twain from the top to the bottom; and the earth did quake, and the rocks rent;" (Matthew 27:50-51)

On the day of crucifixion, the final sacrifice was offered!

There is no evidence in the words or actions of Jesus or those of the Apostles, as recorded in the New Testament, that states or implies that rituals and formality of any religious act, on the part of a person, is a means of accessing the grace and mercy of God. While the ultimate goal of Roman

Catholicism is salvation, the "ceremonial route" is without Biblical foundation. This stands as an irreconcilable difference.

In one commentary about the requirements for Roman Catholics, we read that an individual attains heaven by loving, service, worshipping God and abiding by Church ordinances. This is not supported in any way by scripture or by the action or testimony of Jesus.

The Other Italians accept the premise we can do nothing to attain God's favor, and that it is only through Jesus that an individual receives God's gracious forgiveness. When this happens, the scriptures indicate Jesus will dwell "within man" not on man, next to man, above or underneath him. He is not on an altar or behind an altar. Most of all He is no longer being sacrificed on an altar. He does not dwell in an image or any art form.

The Other Italians rely totally on the Biblical evidence that testifies they have "access to the Father, through the Son."

"My dear children, I am writing this to you so that you will not sin. But if anyone does sin, we have an advocate who pleads our case before the Father. He is Jesus Christ, the one who is truly righteous. He himself is the sacrifice that atones for our sins—and not only our sins but the sins of all the world." (1 John 2:1)

The Other Italians understand that they don't have access through ritual, relic or art form. There is no fear of losing God's favor, and "religious ceremony" is an affront to the One who has already given His Son as the ultimate and final sacrifice. They have learned through the scriptures that you don't have God one minute and lose him the next or have Him one day and not the following day! He promised that He would live in the heart of the forgiven!

There is now nothing to separate them from God. If continuous sacrifices were necessary the rituals of the Old Testament would prevail. Here it is straight from the scriptures in the words of he Apostle Paul: "For I am convinced that neither death, nor life, nor angels, nor principalities, nor things present, nor things to come, nor powers, nor height, nor depth, nor any other created thing, will be able to separate us from the love of God, which is in Christ Jesus our Lord." (Romans 8:38)

To acknowledge that God is in something other than the heart of man is to contradict His own words that proclaim that when a heart is re-born (regenerated) He will dwell within it. This is certainly difficult to comprehend as humans, but it's the testament of scriptures. In reality, we are saying the place where God dwells on earth is in the heart of the one who's regenerated…born from above. Here it is in a letter written to the Christians in the Church at Corinth: "Do you not know that you are a temple of God and that the Spirit of God dwells in you?" (Corinthians 3:16)

The Bible speaks of the body as a "temple" and Jesus Christ…Holy, Omnipotent God…"dwells in our heart by faith" (Ephesians 3:17). To The Other Italians, this is an amazing, marvelous, and awesome truth. It is far beyond the intellectual capacity of the mind that is not rooted in Christ…that is to say have not been born again spiritually. St Paul knew this when he wrote to the Church in Corinth: "But the natural man receiveth not the things of the Spirit of God: for they are foolishness unto him: neither can he know them, because they are spiritually discerned." (I Corinthians 2:14)

According to God's Word, when one believes and receives the Lord Jesus Christ into his or her heart they become, not only one of God's children through their faith in Him, but a sacred place where the Spirit of God dwells.

The Other Italians have their confidence in the promise written in Ephesians 2:8: "For by grace you have been saved through faith; and that not of yourselves, it is the gift of God…"

Chapter Fourteen:
The Ten Commandments

The Other Italians understand why the TEN COMMANDMENTS were given to the children of Israel, and as a result know why Jesus came and died once for the forgiveness of mankind.

The Bible indicates that the children of Israel were an extremely organized society with a sophisticated hierarchy of leaders, and an abundance of civil rules and regulations. They lived under a communal "code of laws" that helped them as a group to exist peacefully as a nation. But Moses recognized that his people were spiritually un-disciplined (unresponsive to the Spirit of God), and could argue away their moral behaviors (much like many people do today). Moses saw his people were self-righteous. God gave him the commandments for some specific reasons. They were detailed to show that man could not attain perfection before God. They center on concerns of the flesh (behavior). Up until this time they were given, there was little understanding and scrutiny of mankind's spiritual depravity. The Law was given to reveal to the individual his or her sin nature that which separated them from God.

The Other Italians understand that their lives are to be governed, not by the Ten Commandments, church laws, religious requirements, and man-made rules but by the Holy Spirit living within them.

One of Jesus' last messages is an eye-opener for most people, including those in the greater Christian world: "Howbeit when he, the Spirit of truth, is come, he will guide you into all truth!" How does something you can't see or feel "speak" to you…let alone lead you? It was a sixteen-word sermon to show how God the Father would deal with the spiritual nature of people. It would confirm (authenticate), condemn (censure) or condone (pardon) behavior in the individual.

The stone tablets are long gone and the writer of the book of Hebrews (Hebrews 8:10) explains where the commandments of God are now contained!

The Ten Commandment tablets were placed in a chest that was known in those days as an "Arc," and while the chest contained the tablets, it was the purpose of God to ultimately dispose of the physical remnants and place the laws somewhere else. The scriptures record the transition:

"You shall love the Lord your God with all your heart and with all your soul and with all your might. These words, which I am commanding you today, shall be on your heart. You shall teach them diligently to your sons and shall talk of them when you sit in your house and when you walk by the way and when you lie down and when you rise up." (Deuteronomy 6:5-7)

"You shall therefore impress these words of mine on your heart and on your soul;" (Deuteronomy 11:18).

"For this commandment which I command you today is not too difficult for you, nor is it out of reach. It is not in heaven, that you should say, 'Who will go up to heaven for us to get it for us and make us hear it, that we may observe it?' Nor is it beyond the sea, that you should say, 'Who will cross the sea for us to get it for us and make us hear it, that we may observe it?' But the word is very near you, in your mouth and in your heart, that you may observe it." (Deuteronomy 30:11-14).

WHERE ARE THE COMMANDMENTS TODAY?

- "The mouth of the righteous utters wisdom, And his tongue speaks justice." "The law of his God is in his heart; His steps do not slip." (Psalm 37:30,31)

- "Your word I have treasured in my heart, That I may not sin against You!" (Psalm 119:11)

- "Do not let kindness and truth leave you; Bind them around your neck, Write them on the tablet of your heart. So you will find favor and good [repute In the sight of God and man. Trust in the Lord with all your heart And do not lean on your own understanding. In all your ways acknowledge Him, And He will make your paths straight." (Proverbs 3:3-6)

- "My son, give attention to my words; Incline your ear to my sayings. Do not let them depart from your sight; Keep them in the midst of your heart. For they are life to those who find them And health to all their body. Watch over your heart with all diligence, For from it flow the springs of life." (Proverbs 4:20-23)

- "My son, keep my words And treasure my commandments within you. Keep my commandments and live, And my teaching as the apple of your eye. Bind them on your fingers; Write them on the tablet of your heart." (Proverbs 7:1-3)

- "Listen to Me, you who know righteousness, A people in whose heart is My law; Do not fear the reproach of man, Nor be dismayed at their revilings." (Isaiah 51:7).

- "For this is the covenant that I will make with the house of Israel After those days, says the Lord: I will put My laws into their minds and I will write them on their hearts. And I will be their God and they shall be My people." (Hebrews 8:10)

No matter what set of laws or decrees or requirements mankind faces, perfection is impossible. There is not one person who has ever kept the commandments except Jesus!

So if our eternal salvation were to be based on keeping the commandments, would anyone be able to receive God's saving grace? The Laws of

God aren't written on tables of stone but are evident in the heart of the regenerated individual!

God's dealing with mankind has moved from an external relationship based on blood offerings to an "internal affair!"

The Other Italians see a simple message in the Holy Scriptures and that message is liberating. When Jesus died on the cross and was resurrected, God would no longer hold our sins against us because Jesus reconciled us to Him.

That means He put us right with God. In the vernacular the words are translated "He squared us with God!"

The Other Italians accept this forgiveness, as completing God's redemptive plan for them, and live their lives in relationship to and with Jesus. They do not live with a list of things they must do or say to attain His favor. Their righteousness before God does not yet need to be attained. No matter how good a person may be, he or she will always fall short in their quest for forgiveness and a relationship with God. It was done in Christ Jesus.

When Jesus came to earth He fulfilled the law, and by his death and resurrection reconciled us to God. This was accomplished when Jesus uttered these words on the Cross - "It is finished!" At that moment the laws of God...the righteousness of God...the precepts or instruction of God were transposed into the heart of the regenerated person.

The Bible does not put out a set of rules to follow to inherit eternal life. Jesus said: "For whosoever will save his life shall lose it: and whosoever will lose his life for my sake shall find it." (St. Matthew 16:25)

One member of this community said this to me in an interview: "Salvation is not a "do it yourself life-long endeavor! It's a "Jesus did it one time thing!" It's hard to believe? Sure, we are human and are looking for the "catch." After all, nothing is free! But the letter to the Ephesians explains the "free gift" guarantee I embrace: "For by grace are ye saved through faith; and that not of yourselves: it is the gift of God: Not of works, lest any man should boast." (Ephesians 2:8-9)

The Other Italians will tell you they have yielded their life to Christ…giving up their will for His will and purpose. For them the requirements for salvation and redemption were completed at a place called Mt. Calvary on a rugged cross. The scriptural record states that when Jesus died on the cross he uttered, in Greek, the word TETELESTAI!

What does the Greek word "tetelestai" mean? Literally translated it means, "It is finished." This word appears in John 19:28 and 19:30. At no point in Jesus' ministry did He ever use these words till he hung on a cross and gave up His life. Here's the account according to Saint John: "After this, when Jesus knew all things were now completed, in order that the scripture might be fulfilled, he said, 'I thirst.'

Two verses later He utters the word Tetelestai!

"Then when he received the sour wine Jesus said, 'It is finished,' and he bowed his head and gave up his spirit."

The word tetelestai was historically used and written on business documents or receipts in New Testament times to indicating that a bill had been paid in full. The Greek-English lexicon by Moulton and Milligan says - "Receipts are often introduced by the phrase tetelestai, usually written in an abbreviated manner." (p. 630)

The connection between receipts and what Christ accomplished would have been quite clear to John's Greek-speaking readership; it would be unmistakable that Jesus Christ had died to pay for their sins (a debt). The Other Italians will tell you that they carry that receipt in their heart!

Chapter Fifteen:
"Hail Mary...Mother of God?

Among the most controversial issues separating The Other Italians from their former religion is the dogma surrounding the status of Mary as a central figure of the Church. Mary has been venerated by the Church fathers as the "Mother of God" and "Mother of the Church." The Other Italians believe this is in direct conflict with the scriptures.

Unbeknown to most parishioners is the fact that there is no reference to Mary being the Mother of God or Mother of the Church in the Holy Scriptures. It was at the Council of Ephesus, which convened more than four hundred years (431 AD) after the birth of Jesus that inaugurated her status.

From that time on, the Virgin Mary was to be called Theotokos, a Greek word that means "God-bearer" (the one who gave birth to God). My interviews revealed a most interesting conflict of thought! Most of those interviewed did not know that Jesus existed from the foundation of the world and that Mary did not pre-exist with God the Father, God the Son and God the Holy Spirit. St. John's Gospel gives quite a revelation: "In the beginning was the Word, and the Word was with God, and the Word was God. The same was in the beginning with God. All things were made by Him; and without Him was not anything made!" JESUS IS THE WORD!

The Other Italians understand that Jesus was right there in the beginning with God. He has always existed! His appearance on earth was only a revelation of whom He was and what He was to do! They certainly reverence Mary but not in the same sense as do Roman Catholics. The ideology of Mary has evolved over the years and so has worship of her as "divinity." They reference the Holy Scriptures for their understanding of Mary's unique role in the birth and life of Jesus.

Today, many Roman Catholics are amazed to learn Mary is referenced only a few times in the entire Bible. One other fact that draws attention, amazement and controversy is the knowledge that Mary had other children.

Jesus' brothers are mentioned in several Bible verses. Matthew 12:46, Luke 8:19, and Mark 3:31, record that day when Jesus' mother and brothers came to see Him. The Bible tells us that Jesus had four brothers: James, Joseph, Simon, and Judas (not the betrayer of course) - (Matthew 13:55). The Bible also confirms that Jesus had sisters; but they are not named or numbered (Matthew 13:56).

In John 7:1-10, His brothers go on to the festival while Jesus stays behind. In Acts 1:14, His brothers and mother are described as praying with the disciples. Later, in Galatians 1:19, it mentions that James was Jesus' brother. The most natural conclusion of these passages is to interpret that Jesus had blood siblings: four brothers and at least two sisters.

Finally, from reading the scriptures, and searching the Church's evolution of her, The Other Italians no longer accept the dogma that Mary was a "perpetual virgin."

Biblical references to Mary are very important as we try to understand whom she was and if she actually played a role in the early church. Mary's interaction with Jesus can be seen in the following events:

- Luke 1:26-38 - The angel Gabriel appears to Mary in Nazareth and tells her that she will conceive a Son by the Holy Spirit.
- Luke 1:39-56 - Mary goes to her relative, Elizabeth.
- Matt. 1:18-24 - Joseph is visited by the Angel Gabriel and told that Mary's conception was by the Holy Spirit. He then marries Mary.

- Luke. 2:1-7 - Matt. 1:25 - Mary and Joseph go to Bethlehem and Jesus is born.
- Luke. 2:8-2 - An angel tells some sheepherders about a Savior being born…Christ the Lord. They go and find Mary and Joseph and the newborn in a stable
- Luke. 2:21-38 Matt. 1:25 - Jesus is circumcised. He is named, and presented in the temple in Jerusalem
- Matt. 2:1-12 - Several years later "Wise Men from the East" visit the family.
- Matt. 2:13-23 - Luke 2:39-40 - King Herod seeks out Jesus so he could kill Him. Joseph takes the family and escapes to Egypt. Later on they return to Israel and take up residence in the City of Nazareth.
- Luke 2:41-51 - At age twelve, the family goes to Jerusalem to celebrate the feast of the Passover.
- Luke 2:51-52 - Jesus continues to grow up in Nazareth.
- John 2:1-11 - Jesus is around thirty years of age and goes with His Disciples to a wedding in Cana. Mary is there too. It is thought that at this time Joseph was deceased.
- John. 2:12 - Jesus, Mary and His brothers make a quick visit Capernaum.
- Matt. 12:46-50 - Mark 3:31-35 - Luke. 8:19-21 -Mary and the brothers of Jesus want an audience with Him while he's teaching in a house at Capernaum.
- John 19:25-27 - Mary was also there at the Crucifixion. "When Jesus therefore saw his mother, and the disciple standing by, whom he loved, he saith unto his mother, Woman, behold thy son! Then saith he to the disciple, Behold thy mother! And from that hour that disciple took her unto his own home."

Many of the references are repeated in the Gospel documentation of Mary)

A BIT OF HISTORY

Jesus was Mary's oldest son and as such, it was his responsibility, under Jewish Law, upon his father's death, to look after his mother in her old age. As he was dying on the cross, He placed his mother in the Disciple John's care. When He told John, "This is thy mother," He was appointing him as her custodian from that day forth. At this point in her life, she went to live in John's house. There is no record that she ever left that house before passing on into eternity. In no way do the scriptures identify, appoint or sanction her as deity or the Mother of all Christians.

The original Catholic Encyclopedia bears this out:

"...Mary was an example and a source of encouragement for the early Christian community. At the same time, it must be confessed that we do not possess any authentic documents bearing directly on Mary's post-Pentecostal life. As to tradition, there is some testimony for Mary's temporary residence in or near Ephesus, but the evidence for her permanent home in Jerusalem is much stronger."

- Acts 1:14 - In an upper room in Jerusalem, we find the apostles, some women, Mary, and the brothers of Jesus praying.
- Gal. 4:4 The mother of Jesus is mentioned in Paul's letter to the Galatians, but not by her name: "But whenthe fullness of the time had come, God sent forth His Son, born of a woman, born under the law."

BUT ISN'T MARY "BLESSED?

Historically the word BLESSED meant "happy!" Women who gave birth in the Old Testament also proclaimed, "Women shall call me blessed" (happy) at the occasion of the birth of a child.

The Other Italians do not limit or diminish the birth of Jesus to Mary; but the Holy Scriptures never elevate her beyond her human status. Mary was selected to bear Jesus. She must have been a wonderful young girl. Speculation is that she might have been as young as thirteen. At any age, she surely was an intelligent, obedient and humble person. The Other Italians see her in this light...blessed (happy), but not superior to others.

A scripture passage bears record and definitive testimony to Mary's place in the ministry of Jesus. One day while preaching there was incident in the streets: "And it came to pass, as he spake these things, a certain woman of the company lifted up her voice, and said unto him, Blessed is the womb that bare thee, and the paps which thou hast sucked! (Luke 11-26)

There's no denying a woman called Mary "blessed" but Jesus responds quickly: "But even more blessed are all who hear the word of God and put it into practice."

Jesus actually censures this woman and shows the importance of obedience to the Word of God. On another occasion He speaks to the status of people in the Kingdom: "Verily I say unto you, among them that are born of women there hath not risen a greater than John the Baptist: notwithstanding he that is least in the kingdom of heaven is greater than he." (Matthew 11:11)

Here Jesus indicates that John the Baptist is great…but the least in the Kingdom of God. Jesus elevated no man or woman at any time.

The History of Mary's deification points to the influence of other cultures and religions.

Here are excerpts from an article by researcher Carissa Cegavskel, who is a renowned expert on the - "Goddesses of the Ancient World!"

Theotokos: "How the Mother Goddess became Mary!"

"Mary becomes Mother of God: The year 431 A.D. was a momentous one in the history of the Queen of Heaven. That's the year the church fathers, meeting in Ephesus in modern day Turkey, officially declared that Mary is Theotokos, literally, in Greek, the one who gave birth to God. More commonly her title is paraphrased as Mother of God. This was an important political step, as it clarified for the theologians that Jesus was both God and man. Perhaps just as importantly, however, it pacified the people, who were demanding that Mary be acknowledged as a divinity. (Mary's deification is rooted in the wishes of people and Church "officials" who succumb to their demands. Most ancient religions had female gods and the idea of a God or Goddess of Heaven was common among their beliefs).

(The real issue at hand was that there was a need to clarify and establish that Jesus was the Son of God and the Son of Man).

Technically, the church denied Mary as divine, as a Goddess, but in practical terms, it conveyed a sense of holiness which made her a viable rival to the other popular Roman/Greek/Egyptian hybrids Goddess of the time, represented variously as Diana, Cybele, and Isis. As a result of their decision, Mary's divinity has been able to shine through in art and writing and devotion of those who love her.

Beautiful artwork throughout the world depicts Mary holding her infant son exactly as Isis had done for thousands of years before her.

Many people pray to this Queen of Heaven to intercede for them and miraculous cures and protections of entire countries in war are attributed to her and to her icons. The Vladimir Madonna.... is, for example, said to have saved Russia from Tamerlane in 1395, the Tatars in the 15th century, and even from Germany in World War II.

A similar icon in Cosenza, Italy, has a spot which is said to represent the icon's having absorbed the plague in the 16th Century and protected the city's residents from that dread disease. Here is a copy of what is claimed to be a very ancient prayer to Mary, dating to perhaps the 2nd or 3rd century:

"We turn to you for protection,   Holy Mother of God   Listen to our prayers   and help us in our needs. Save us from every danger, glorious and blessed Virgin."

How did Christianity take over the West? It started about 100 years before the church fathers met in Ephesus, when the emperor of a then united Rome, Emperor Constantine, converted after a successful battle which he attributed to intervention by the Christians' God. The whole of Rome was converted officially under the later Emperor Theodosius in 391 AD. Then the empire split into eastern and western halves in 395 AD. The eastern empire was ruled from Constantinople, a city that had earlier been founded by Constantine (hence the name) as a Christian city. Much later, in the 11th century, the religion of the east, including Greece, Turkey, and southeastern Europe, was to split from Roman Catholicism, becoming the Eastern Orthodox Church. Orthodox worshipers, like Catholics, venerate Mary.

In the year 431, though, the church was still more or less united and the church fathers met for the Third Ecumenical Council in Ephesus. Every time they met like this, theological ideas would be made into official dogma, churches with different theological ideas would be declared heretics and some churches would peel off from "mainstream" Christianity and generally fade into obscurity. This time, 250 bishops showed up to vote on whether Jesus was God and man both at the same time and, hence, whether Mary was literally the Mother of God. The pro-Theotokos (Mother of God) faction was backed, not surprisingly, by the Egyptians, who venerated images of Mary reminiscent of those of Isis. Bribes were given and fighting ensued in the streets in the lead-up to the bishops' vote on this question. They voted yes, a group called the Nestorians went home really mad (also, heretics), and the crowds went wild, cheering in the streets when the vote was announced.

Constantine ruled from the years 306 – 327 and saw the need to pacify his citizens' various and many religious beliefs. It was his task to have a unified and stable kingdom. Much like today, countries are looking for stability less they slowly disintegrate and follow the path of ancient Rome; and religion still plays a part in their cultural battles. One of his goals was to unite Christianity with pagan worship practices. He was a "sun-worshipper!"

Historical records show his devotion: "On the venerable Day of the Sun let the magistrates and people residing in cities rest, and let all workshops be closed." (March 7, 321).

He made this decree in honor of the sun after his supposed conversion to Christianity. The inscription on his coins read: "SOL INVICTO COMITI" (Committed to the Invincible Sun). He devised a simple strategy to further stabilize his citizenry by bringing together the Roman Church and his pagan beliefs. The easiest way to bring harmony would be to blend sun worship and Christianity; so for starters the priests of Mithra (Zoroastrian Deity) would be become the priests of the Roman church and the priestesses that were in the Cybele Temples (Anatolian Cult) nuns of the Roman church.

The blending of "religions" found its reality in the worship of a mother goddess…the one thing the pagan community would not give up.

Constantine and his religious leaders decided that Mary the mother of Jesus could replace the pagan mothers. People would still pray to their mother goddess…but call her MARY instead of Cybele, Semiramis, Rhea and Isis. These were the names the other Queens of heaven were known by. The result was achieved. Names and worship attributed to their pagan mother was transferred to the most important woman in the Bible…MARY.

The revelation of historical records like this has brought The Other Italians to the point of rejecting "theoretical ideas," the "theology based on will of the masses," "adoption of pagan beliefs and practices," and creating and adopting theology on the basis of political expediency."

Few Roman Catholics I interviewed were aware that their "religion" has adopted and integrated pagan rituals.

Pagan worship ideas are Satanic when seen through the illumination of the scriptures. Key to this is that Jesus did not come to blend in with pagan cultures or adopt the cultural traditions of nations.

The Bible says: "the one who practices sin is of the devil; for the devil has sinned from the beginning. The Son of God appeared for this purpose, to destroy the works of the devil." (1 John 3:8)

The Other Italians do not believe you get to God by adopting and adapting man-made religious rituals, and nowhere in the scriptures is there any reference to Mary being an intercessor or one who has access to God in heaven. This is then their profession of their faith: "And there is salvation in no one else, for there is no other name under heaven given among men by which we must be saved." (Acts 4:12)

Chapter Sixteen:
Communion and Confirmation

HOLY COMMUNION - The celebration of the first Communion (sacrament) is a milestone in the life of the child whose family practices the Roman Catholic Religion.

After receiving communion the child can receive the "Host" - being the body of Jesus Christ.

On the other hand, The Other Italians believe a child can participate in a communion service when he or she reaches an age where they understand their need for a Savior and make a profession of faith. Usually a parent or guardian looks for the following:

- The child has an understanding that that the bread and wine (elements) have no saving grace and that they are symbolic.
- The child has spoken (made) a profession of faith that indicates he/she understand that Jesus wants to be their Savior and that they earnestly desire to ask Him into their heart and life. This must not be perceived as a religious ceremony but a confession of faith, that their sin separates them from God.
- The child demonstrates a convincing declaration of faith and obedience to the teachings of the Bible that the communion table is for a

time of looking back on the death of Jesus with an understanding of why He died for them.

- The child shows obedience and love for God by their words, actions and their behavior in the home, at school and play.
- The child explains the significance of the (sacrament) communion ceremony and that it is a commemorative sacrament as a reminder of the death of Jesus?
- The Other Italians are aware that they cannot set a date or time for this spiritual juncture, thus they teach, encourage and set a living example for their child to follow.

Much of the instruction given to a child in the Roman Catholic Faith is not accepted as Biblical by The Other Italians.

The following is taught in preparation for a Roman Catholic child's first communion. (Catholic Parent Magazine: Four Ways To Help Prepare Your Child For First Communion).

1. "The Eucharist is a meal. On the table of the altar, Jesus feeds us with his Body and Blood, under the appearances of bread and wine." (The Other Italians believe the bread and wine are symbols and not the actual body and blood of Jesus).

2. "Just as food nourishes our bodies, the Eucharist is spiritual food that nourishes our soul." (The Other Italians do not teach that the sacrament is a substitute or spiritual food). In St. John's Gospel 4:34 Jesus tells His disciples: "My meat is to do the will of him that sent me, and to finish his work."

3. "The bread and wine are signs that tell us the Lord is nourishing us spiritually." (The Other Italians hold to the Biblical declarations that Jesus is: Our savior, helper, healer, intermediary, advocate, substitute, provider, peace and much more. The Other Italians teach their children to rely on the person of Jesus for the needs of their life, and that no ceremony bestows or grants God's provision for or to them. They teach this is a real happening that was accomplished once and for all mankind.

4. "Unlike other signs--stop signs, for example--that can't cause us to do anything, the bread and wine of the Eucharist cause what they signify. They nourish us in our spirit; they cause us to grow in Christ." (The Other Italians hold to the scriptures as a base for their understanding of the Holy Spirit in the life of the individual. The promise Jesus made to the Disciples is that His spirit would live on IN them. They believe as you yield to the voice of truth within you…you grow in faith and grace!)

"Thus it is written, and thus it behooved Christ to suffer, and to rise from the dead the third day: And that repentance and remission of sins should be preached in his name among all nations, beginning at Jerusalem. And ye are witnesses of these things. And, behold, I send the promise of my Father upon you: but tarry ye in the city of Jerusalem, until ye be endued with power from on high." -- Luke 24:46-49

Nowhere in the scriptures does Jesus say or promote that His divine presence is more near or evident in the bread or wine or at any juncture during the formal communion. The message of the Gospel is that Jesus came to dwell within the regenerated man and woman. That dwelling is permanent.

The Other Italians do not believe the bread and wine are vehicles of God's saving grace. If that were the case, then a person would have to return again and again to receive it as is the case with practicing Roman Catholics. They teach their children that they must exercise a simple faith that Jesus can and will forgive them for the sin- and come to live within them because of their regenerated spirit.

They believe when Jesus rose from the dead as recorded in John 20:21-22 the Holy Spirit was manifested thereby "filling" them. "Then said Jesus to them again, Peace be unto you: as my Father hath sent me, even so send I you. And when he had said this, he breathed on them, and saith unto them, Receive ye the Holy Ghost:" The Other Italians view the communion elements as symbolic and spiritual (not physical or material). Again, their children are not taught that the bread is the body of Jesus and the wine His blood.

CONFIRMATON

The Other Italians do not practice the "rite" or ritual of confirmation. They do not classify it as a sacrament, although there are non-catholic religious denominations that require some type of "inauguration" for a person to become a member of the congregation. In short, they believe a child should come to an age of reasoning before they enter into an independent status (membership) in the local church they attend.

Chapter Seventeen:
Statues and Statutes

STATUES

While commentaries indicate that Roman Catholics do not worship statues, my interviews with The Other Italians, confirmed that in the past, perhaps by ignorance of their Church's doctrine, they did reverence and actually worship the statues in their church or those they saw in other settings.

Typical of the answers Roman Catholic parishioners offered this author regarding this "misconception" of those outside of the Church have about "worshipping statues,' was as following: "We do not pray to the statue. We pray in front of the statue and use it as a symbol, kind of to help us visualize whom we are praying to. And even then we do not worship the person the statue depicts, we honor that person, and ask them to intercede for us."

Roman Catholic Canonical law clarifies the use of "images" in worship:

IV. "YOU SHALL NOT MAKE FOR YOURSELF A GRAVEN IMAGE…" (2129) The divine injunction included the prohibition of every representation of God by the hand of man. Deuteronomy explains: "Since you saw no form on the day that the Lord spoke to you at Horeb out of the midst of the fire, beware lest you act corruptly by making a graven image for yourselves, in the form of any figure..." (66) It is the absolutely transcendent God who revealed himself to Israel. "He is the all," but at the same time "he is greater than all his works." (67) (Mt. Horeb is where Moses received the Ten Commandments)

There is no question that images were created in the Old Testament and much of the argument for the creation and reverence is based on those that might have been used in worship during past ages. The Arc of the Covenant, for instance, where the tablets containing the Ten Commandment were kept (Made famous by the movie: Raiders of the Lost Ark), was ordained and designed by God. It had "Cherubim" angels on top of the casing but they were never used for worship in any sense, but served as an adorning ornament.

And something happened when Jesus came to earth! The New Testament references, according to Bible believing Christians, such as The Other Italians, indicate that Jesus is the "likeness of God." The scriptures testify to this in Colossians 1:15: "He is the image of the invisible God..." As such, no representation in art, music, design or other man-conceived items are necessary to bring God to our worship and life. Here is the Bible on the issue: "Being then the children of God, we ought not to think that the Divine Nature is like gold or silver or stone, an image formed by the art and thought of man." (Acts 17:29)

There is no question that physical art forms like pictures, icons and statues exist within the Roman Catholic Church; most Catholic theologians will state that they are representative of the person depicted, and help to focus the individual on them. In doing so, the member prays in the anticipation the one represented will intercede for them in heaven.

Who would question the feelings one gets when they enter a cathedral, mansion or see a magnificent landscape? However, the issues of prayer and worship demand clarification from the scriptures. The Other Italians reference these, not in defense or argument, but explanation as to what happened to the world when Jesus physically came, lived, died and was resurrected: "And Christ became a human being and lived here on earth among us and was full of loving forgiveness and truth. And some of us have seen his glory the glory of the only Son of the heavenly Father!" It was Peter who declared: "You are the Christ, the SON OF THE LIVING GOD!"

WHERE IS GOD AND WHERE DOES GOD DWELL?

The message of the scriptures is that we can go directly to God through Jesus. The great misunderstanding that non-Catholics have about Catholics who contend they "pray to statues," is not about what they do or what the image represents, as much as the question: Where is God?

Does a person have to go to someone to intercede on his or her behalf? Is God unapproachable? Can man actually communicate with Him?

Here's what the Bible answers: "…in whom you also are being built together into a dwelling of God in the Spirit." The Living Bible reads: "And you also are joined with him and with each other by the Spirit and are part of this dwelling place of God. (Ephesians 2:22)

The writer of the Book of Acts wrote: "the Most High does not dwell in houses made by human hands." (Acts 7:48)

The message within the Gospel and Epistles declares that Jesus lives within the individual; while it might a "dutiful route" for some to pray through images, for the regenerated individual this is without scriptural justification. For them, Jesus lives within and they need no representation or image to make them mindful of Him. The promise of the scriptures, in the words of Jesus, is that He would dwell within. "Do you not know that you are a temple of God and that the Spirit of God dwells in you?" (1 Corinthians 3:16)

One of my interviewees addressed this issue with an illustration: "My own take on this subject leads me back to an experience I had when I was a young teacher. The children in my school wrote a long letter of invitation to the President of the United States. Three hundred signatures at the bottom of the letter indicated their desire to see him up close and personal. The administration sent the letter with little anticipation he would actually come. They guessed right! A large life-like placard with his image came off of the UPS truck. The announcement was made over the public address system and you could hear the sighs of disappoint throughout the classes and halls. So we had the physical image…but not President. A few days later the Principal actually received a phone call from the White House. He was coming! Security around the building and in town was unbelievable. The kids actually got to meet him, shake his hand and ask questions.

When you think about it, the images of the Old Testament were representations. When Jesus arrived in Bethlehem, the world got the real thing. After the President showed up, the placard had no meaning and was given a resting place in the custodian's office for few months. It was finally "removed" permanently but not before yours truly posed for a picture with it in the hall before it left the building. No image could ever substitute for the one thing I got to do. A few months before I actually shook his hand!"

The images in the Old Testament were shadows or symbols of things that would actually, someday come to pass. You might consider that the Old Testament chronicles a journey Adam took over a period of thousands of years, finally arriving in Bethlehem, with his journey ending at an empty tomb. During that journey there was a temple and God did dwell therein; but when Jesus came, no temple could ever contain the glory of God…except a regenerated individual.

Bowing and praying before a statue, is an important ritual within the Church. The Roman Catholic Canon (2132) acknowledges the veneration of those portrayed in images. "The honor rendered to a an image passes to its prototype…and whoever venerates an image venerates the person portrayed in it." (70) The honor paid to sacred images is a "respectful veneration," not the adoration due to God alone:

It sounds reasonable and "logically religious" but there is no foundation for such ritual in the Bible.

The Other Italians believe if you can go directly to the Father, through the Son, why would any intermediary, symbol, statue or icon be necessary to approach Him? "And when you are praying, do not use meaningless repetition as the Gentiles do, for they suppose that they will be heard for their many words…So do not be like them; for your Father knows what you need before you ask Him." (Matthew 6:7-8)

Roman Catholic interviewees explained that statues were a "source of contact" between God and them." Subsequent interviews with Roman Catholic constituents indicated that they do "worship and pray to statues." Today, The Other Italians hold to the scripture and the context thereof in the Bible as it relates to imagery of God. The scriptures are clear on the issue of representational statues, pictures and things crafted: "Ye shall make you no idols nor graven image, neither rear you up a standing image, neither shall ye set up any image of stone in your land, to bow down unto it: for I am the Lord your God." (Leviticus 26:1)

When He came to earth, Jesus became the visual image of God. While we don't have an actual reflection of Him, the Bible believing Christian is aware of the nature of God and worship as explained in the scriptures and will state: "Our worship of God, through Jesus is spiritual." The physical property of statues is solid and temporal. St. Paul wrote in his letter to the church in Colossae: "He is the image of the invisible God, the firstborn of all creation." (Colossians 1:15)

The Apostle declares Jesus is the physical image of God.

St. John 1:18 reads: "No one has ever seen God, but the one and only Son, who is himself God and is in closest relationship with the Father, has made him known." Here is that verse in the Living Bible: "No one has ever actually seen God, but, of course, his only Son has, for he is the companion of the Father and has told us all about him."

The Other Italians do not seek God through any medium other than by the Holy Spirit dwelling within them. They also state that at one time they thought they had "spiritual feelings about God" when they gazed at images, entered beautiful structures and in events that had them enjoying nature. Such things made them "feel" close to God, but in reality, when the image was gone they said they felt nothing. Today, their prayers are addressed to God, through the Son…Jesus Christ!

STATUTES OR BIBLICAL TRUTH

There are literally thousands of statutes (laws) that govern the affairs of the Roman Catholic Church. These are known as "Canon Laws," and are an evolving and changing code of ecclesiastical (religious) laws governing the Catholic Church.

The Wikipedia explanation confirms: "In the Roman Church, universal positive ecclesiastical laws, based upon either immutable divine and natural law, or changeable circumstantial and merely positive law, derive formal authority and promulgation from the office of pope, who as Supreme Pontiff possesses the totality of legislative, executive, and judicial power in his person. The actual subject material of the canons is not just doctrinal or moral in nature, but all-encompassing of the human condition."

The Other Italians take exception to the unilateral or independent jurisdiction of one man…the Pope. They view it as not Biblical because there is no mention of a "Pope" in the scriptures or authority given to any one person to be the sole interpreter of scriptures. Ideas like "changeable circumstances" have made the Roman Catholic Church doctrine subject to change. In the process, The Other Italians believe altering and eliminating that which at one time, were edicts, sanctions and revelations, resulting in requirements and obligations for worship, is inconsistent with the immutable content in the Holy Scriptures. This is an irreconcilable difference.

BUT WHAT ABOUT THE BIBLE

The Bible is not to be viewed as intellectual. It is the revelation of God to mankind through His servants He has chosen throughout history. It is God who selects the times and ways by which He discloses His message to mankind, and not a delegate. The Other Italians accept that the canon of scriptures is complete.

Consider the words of the writer of the book of Hebrews and his summation: "God, who at sundry times and in divers manners spake in time past unto the fathers by the prophets, Hath in these last days spoken unto us by his Son, whom he hath appointed heir of all things, by whom also he made the worlds" (Heb. 1:1, 2).

The Other Italians know the consequences of man's intervention with the scriptures because there are cautions threaded throughout regarding the adding or deleting from it.

"And if any man shall take away from the words of the book of this prophecy, God shall take away his part out of the book of life, and out of the holy city, and from the things which are written in this book." (Revelation 22:19)

Perhaps the old farmer said it in a crude way, but what he said is a testimony to the impact the Bible has had on individuals of all ages and cultures: "If it ain't in the Bible…it ain't!"

The Apostle Paul was a little more sophisticated and wrote this: "For me to live is Christ…to die is gain!" (Philippians 1:21)

Chapter Eighteen:
Papal Succession – Church Leadership

The Roman Catholic Church holds to the belief that their leader, the Pope, must follow an "unbroken" line or succession of men originating with St. Peter and leading to the present. There are Protestant church groups that also affirm this tradition in terms of the appointment of their clergy as well. This succession cannot be broken at any point as it insures the integrity and fidelity of the office. To be an authentic Pope, one must follow in an uncompromised line from the throne of St. Peter.

The Ritual of Papal Succession transfers the all-inclusive powers of the office, pertaining to the governance of the Church: Executive, Judicial, and Legislative. The Pope has absolute power! But the individual can only hold the office, and the authority thereof, if he is a direct descendent of St. Peter through ordination. With such ordination, it is believed he acts in the place of Christ here on earth. The position of "Pope" is one that stands in supremacy to all Roman Catholics and members believe he is "infallible!" However, while the Church maintains the legacy of an uninterrupted and uncompromised succession, there is evidence that during certain documented periods in history the Papal line was indeed broken at least seven times.

The Other Italians question this ordinance and the necessity of Papal succession or any historical leadership succession in the New Testament

Church as it has no Biblical basis. Their faith is based on conviction, individual responsibility, and commitment. Above all, they do not accept or believe that the Pope is "Infallible" or that he or anyone else is the "Vicar of God!"

As for chronological integrity, it has been documented that during the period spanning 65 CE to 891 CE (approximately 559 years), there was no Christian (Pope) or even Pagan high priest in Rome.

The major breaks in succession occurred during these periods of time:

- 65 to 193 CE
- 222 to 309 CE
- 310 to 366 CE
- 452 to 536 CE
- 590 to 751 CE
- 847 to 872 CE
- 876 to 891 CE

(Note CE ="Christian Era" - an alternative to "Anno Domini or AD")

The Other Italians do not accept the origination or transference of "headship with ecclesiastical power" through papal succession within the New Testament Church. They declare Christ is the head of the Church and that the scriptures are void of any inference or any specific text stating an individual or organization was ordained to assume the "role of Christ" when the Lord departed. There is no scripture that says He ever transferred his divine leadership to man!

In his departing sermon Jesus preached this: "But when He, the Spirit of truth, comes, He will guide you into all the truth; for He will not speak on His own initiative, but whatever He hears, He will speak; and He will disclose to you what is to come. He will glorify Me, for He will take of Mine and will disclose it to you. All things that the Father has are Mine; therefore I said that He takes of Mine and will disclose it to you." (John 16:13-15)

The Other Italians believe Christians can know the truths of God by praying, reading the Bible and submitting to the "voice of the Holy Spirit, who dwells within them. The promise of Jesus was that the Spirit of God would reside within and guide (some interpretations translate "lead") the individual into ALL truth.

Nowhere in the Bible is anyone or any institution, whether it is a singular church, denomination or international religious organization, given the authority or singular right to discern the scriptures for an individual. In the Roman Catholic Church, only under the authority of the Pope are scriptures to be interpreted. Paragraph 100 of the Roman Catholic Catechism reads:

The following quote is from Paragraph 100 in the Catholic Catechism: "The task of interpreting the Word of God authentically has been entrusted solely to the Magisterium of the Church, that is, to the Pope and to the bishops in communion with him."

This message for the New Testament "believer" is engraved (contained) in the scriptures and testifies to the power within the individual to know the scriptures: 1 Corinthians 2:16 - For who hath known the mind of the Lord, that he may instruct him? But we have the mind of Christ.

- Romans 12:2 - And be not conformed to this world: but be ye transformed by the renewing of your mind, that ye may prove what is that good, and acceptable, and perfect, will of God.
- 1 Corinthians 2:14-16 - But the natural man receiveth not the things of the Spirit of God: for they are foolishness unto him: neither can he know them, because they are spiritually discerned."
- Philippians 2:5 - Let this mind be in you, which was also in Christ Jesus."
- Matthew 28:18 – "And Jesus came and spake unto them, saying, All power is given unto me in heaven and in earth." (God does not share His power with man)
- 1 John 2:6 - He that saith he abideth in him ought himself also so to walk, even as he walked.
- 1 Peter 1:13 – "Wherefore gird up the loins of your mind, be sober, and hope to the end for the grace that is to be brought unto you at the revelation of Jesus Christ;"

- Hebrews 11:6 – "But without faith it is impossible to please him: for he that cometh to God must believe that he is, and that he is a rewarder of them that diligently seek him."
- 2 Timothy 3:16 – "All scripture is given by inspiration of God, and is profitable for doctrine, for reproof, for correction, for instruction in righteousness:"
- 2 Timothy 3:5 – "Having a form of godliness, but denying the power thereof: from such turn away."
- 2 Timothy 1:7 – "For God hath not given us the spirit of fear; but of power, and of love, and of a sound mind."
- 1 Corinthians 2:13-16 –"Which things also we speak, not in the words which man's wisdom teaches, but which the Holy Ghost teaches; comparing spiritual things with spiritual."
- Romans 8:9 – "But ye are not in the flesh, but in the Spirit, if so be that the Spirit of God dwell in you. Now if any man have not the Spirit of Christ, he is none of his."
- Romans 8:1-39 –"There is therefore now no condemnation to them which are in Christ Jesus, who walk not after the flesh, but after the Spirit."
- John 16:15 – "All things that the Father hath are mine: therefore said I, that he shall take of mine, and shall show it unto you."
- John 5:24 – "Verily, verily, I say unto you, He that heareth my word, and believeth on him that sent me, hath everlasting life, and shall not come into condemnation; but is passed from death unto life.
- John 3:16 – "For God so loved the world, that he gave his only begotten Son, that whosoever believeth in him should not perish, but have everlasting life."
- John 3:3 – "Jesus answered and said unto him, Verily, verily, I say unto thee, Except a man be born again, he cannot see the kingdom of God." (A spiritual birth)
- 1 John 5:20 – "And we know that the Son of God is come, and hath given us an understanding, that we may know him that is true, and we are in him that is true, even in his Son Jesus Christ. This is the true God, and eternal life."

- 2 Corinthians 5:17 – "Therefore if any man be in Christ, he is a new creature: old things are passed away; behold, all things are become new."
- Matthew 10:20 – "For it is not ye that speak, but the Spirit of your Father which speaks in you."

The Other Italians accept the finality of the scriptures that indicate the "Holy Spirit," within them, leads to all truth, and that nothing can be added to assist in the process. Thus, the Bible becomes their guide.

While The Other Italians reject the idea of a supreme and authoritative leader, the Bible does outline a schema for church leadership. The station of POPE is not mentioned therein.

The Apostle Paul delineated a simple description and criteria for leadership in the local church. The Epistles of the New Testament chronicle the ministry of the early church, and spell out these leadership roles and responsibilities. The Apostle Paul never addresses, announces or specifies the role or station of an absolute head in his letters, and while St. Peter is said to be the first link in the succession of Popes, he plays a much lesser role as a minister to the churches than he.

Within the Pauline Epistles (Those written by St. Paul) we see the formation of the early churches that began to be scattered in the then known world. It was St. Paul, with the inspiration and leading of the Holy Spirit, who identified two leadership positions to bring structure and order to these local assemblies. The leadership titles are as follows:

CHRIST IS THE HEAD OF THE CHURCH

The Bible indicates there are two main sanctioned designations of leaders for the New Testament Church. Two leadership roles are identified: ELDER AND DEACON. The qualifications for both are the same and they are delineated in St. Paul's letter to Timothy (1 Timothy 3:8-12). Nowhere in the Word of God is there a policy of "succession" for those who would be elected or appointed to these roles by the local congregation.

QUALIFICATIONS

Those chosen to lead must be, do and have the following:

- Dignified (v. 8): The usual meaning for this word is: honorable, respectable, esteemed, or worthy, and is closely related to "respectable."
- Not double-tongued (v. 8): They must be examples of what they say to the congregation. Their words must be trusted, and be creditable.
- Not addicted to too much wine (v. 8): A man is disqualified for the office of deacon if he is addicted to wine or other strong drink. They must have self-control and be self-disciplined.
- Not greedy for dishonest gain (v. 8): Since part of their responsibility is to handle the finances of the church, they must not be lovers of money.
- Sound in faith and life (v. 9): Paul also indicates that a deacon must "hold the mystery of the faith with a clear conscience holding firm the true gospel without wavering. His behavior must be consistent with his beliefs.
- Blameless (v. 10): "Blameless" is a general term referring to a person's overall character. Although Paul does not specify what type of testing is to take place, at a minimum, the candidate's personal background, reputation, and theological positions should be examined. Moreover, the congregation should not only examine a potential deacon's moral, spiritual, and doctrinal maturity, but should also consider the person's work in the church. Newcomers off the street, no matter how convincing must be proven before being selected to serve.
- Godly wife (v. 11 - refers to a deacon's wife or to a deaconess. According to Paul, deacons' wives must "be dignified, not slanderers, but sober-minded, faithful in all things" (v. 11). Like her husband, the wife must be dignified or respectable. Secondly, she must not be a slanderer or a person who goes around spreading gossip. A deacon's wife must also be sober-minded or temperate. That is, she must be able to make good judgments and must not be involved in things that might hinder such judgment. Finally, she must be "faithful in all things" (cf. 1 Tim. 5:10). This is a general requirement that functions similarly to the requirement for elders to be "above reproach and for deacons to be "blameless"
- Husband of one wife (v. 12) -refers to the faithfulness of a husband toward his wife. The dictate is there must be no other woman in his

life to whom he relates in an intimate way either emotionally or physically.

- Manage children and household well (v. 12): A deacon must be the spiritual leader of his wife and children.

The Other Italians attend churches where these Biblical standards are held high for the local leadership.

ROLE OF THE ELDERS – Elders in the church are to deal with the spiritual issues involving the spiritual life and welfare of the members. The role of the Elder is to emanate the scriptures by their lives and work. They are to be examples of holiness and goodness, spiritually alive and given to prayer.

ROLE OF THE DEACONS –Deacons are to attend to the daily operations of the church and the physical needs of the members. While there is no additional or lesser job description listed, they are to assist the Elders by dealing with the finances, building, membership needs and general duties.

The Other Italians follow the scriptures in all matters pertaining to the guidance of the local congregation. In some denominations there are other designations for leaders, but the intent of their office is to serve as a spiritual leader where they teach, counsel and conduct the affairs of the church. They possess no divine power to rule over the corporate body of Christ. Again, they accept that the Biblical declaration that Christ and He alone is the Head of the Church

It appears that man's best intentions to maintain traditions, cultural rites and religious beliefs, are subject to many influences. Regarding Papal Succession, there are historical records that indicate that on more than one occasion the person chosen to be Pope came by the position in "unorthodox," even "heretical" ways.

Until this generation could access the World-Wide-Web, this information was not readily available. The "Conclave" (popularized by Hollywood movie-makers and Media) is a closed-door convention whereby Church Cardinals meet and vote. But what was supposed to be a highly spiritual event, guaranteeing succession, sometimes was compromised by the influence by Roman Emperors and Kings. Prior to 1059 there is evidence that Popes were indeed appointed by these secular leaders, thereby compromising "papal succession."

Throughout history the Church was unfortunately linked to the cultural and political arena whereby it yielded its powers to Godless demagogues and tyrants, and they chose the one to sit on "St. Peter's throne." The historical record confirms this to have happened on many occasions. Again, researching the web yields information about these occurrences.

The Other Italians are respectful of those in ministerial office, but find no Biblical mandate for any leadership succession to validate their title or role. There is one succession that the scriptures affirm: "The Spirit Himself testifies with our spirit that we are children of God, and if children, heirs also, heirs of God and fellow heirs with Christ, if indeed we suffer with Him so that we may also be glorified with Him." (Romans 8:16-1)

Chapter Nineteen:
The Place Called Heaven

When asked if he actually believed there was a real heaven, the old timer sitting on the bench in front of a general store in small town on Route 66 answered, "Well I sure don't want to die before I find out!"

The subjects of dying, death and heaven prompt many to hold on to the idea of reincarnation in the hope that there is an after-life. I'm sure it won't surprise you that given the choice, my interviewees all chose heaven over hell. The subject can be very confusing, but not for The Other Italians.

The Born Again Christian references the Bible and what it has to say about the "hereafter!" While the topics of heaven and hell prompt jokes, riddles, research and all that goes with the "unknown," the Bible makes clear that there is a hell and there is a heaven! The vast majority of the people I interviewed did not know for sure they'd get to heaven some day. The Other Italians accept only the declarations of the scriptures that are not void in dealing with the topic. The Bible begins with an explanation and a promise:

- "In the beginning God created the heavens and the earth." Genesis 1:1 Unbeknown to most people is the fact that Jesus came down from heaven. His birth in Bethlehem was not His beginning. He came from heaven with a promise for those who identified and accepted Him as "Christ, the Son of the Living God!" "I am the bread of life; whoever comes to me shall not hunger, and whoever believes in me shall never thirst. But I said to you that you have seen me and yet do not believe. All that the Father gives me will come to me, and whoever comes to me I will never cast out. For I have come down from heaven, not to do my own will but the will of him who sent me. And this is the will of him who sent me, that I should lose nothing of all that he has given me, but raise it up on the last day. For this is the will of my Father, that everyone who looks on the Son and believes in him should have eternal life, and I will raise him up on the last day." (John 1:14; John 6:35-40)

- Jesus told the Disciples of the provisions He had made for them in heaven. "In my Father's house are many rooms. If it were not so, would I have told you that I go to prepare a place for you?" (John 14:2)

- Jesus returned to heaven after His resurrection: "And He led them out as far as Bethany, and He lifted up His hands and blessed them. While He was blessing them, He parted from them and was carried up into heaven. And they, after worshiping Him, returned to Jerusalem with great joy, and were continually in the temple praising God!" (Luke 24:50-53)

- Jesus is now in heaven, seated with the Father: "we have such a high priest, who has taken His seat at the right hand of the throne of the Majesty in the heavens." (Hebrews 8:1)

- Our mortal body is a temporary dwelling place. "For we know that if the earthly tent which is our house is torn down, we have a building from God, a house not made with hands, eternal in the heavens. For indeed in this house we groan, longing to be clothed with our dwelling from heaven, inasmuch as we, having put it on, will not be found naked. For indeed while we are in this tent, we groan, being burdened, because we do not want to be unclothed but to be clothed, so that what is mortal will be swallowed up by life. Now He who prepared us for this very purpose is God, who gave to us the Spirit as a pledge."

Here it is in the Living Bible:

"For we know that when this tent we live in now is taken down—when we die and leave these bodies—we will have wonderful new bodies in heaven, homes that will be ours forevermore, made for us by God himself and not by human hands. How weary we grow of our present bodies. That is why we look forward eagerly to the day when we shall have heavenly bodies that we shall put on like new clothes. For we shall not be merely spirits without bodies. These earthly bodies make us groan and sigh, but we wouldn't like to think of dying and having no bodies at all. We want to slip into our new bodies so that these dying bodies will, as it were, be swallowed up by everlasting life. This is what God has prepared for us, and as a guarantee he has given us his Holy Spirit." (2 Corinthians 5:1-5)

- The "spiritually regenerated" person can indeed look forward to heaven: St John affirmed: "Then I saw a new heaven and a new earth; for the first heaven and the first earth passed away, and there is no longer any sea. And I saw the holy city, new Jerusalem, coming down out of heaven from God, made ready as a bride adorned for her husband. And I heard a loud voice from the throne, saying, "Behold, the tabernacle of God is among men, and He will dwell among them, and they shall be His people, and God Himself will be among them and He will wipe away every tear from their eyes; and there will no longer be any death; there will no longer be any mourning, or crying, or pain; the first things have passed away." (Rev.21:1-4)
- The Bible promises an instant change for those who "walk by faith." "Therefore, being always of good courage, and knowing that while we are at home in the body we are absent from the Lord— for we walk by faith, not by sight— we are of good courage, I say, and prefer rather to be absent from the body and to be at home with the Lord." (2 Corinthians 5:8)
- The beauty and majesty of Heaven is beyond our reasoning: "But, as it is written, - What no eye has seen, nor ear heard, nor the heart of man imagined, what God has prepared for those who love him." (1 Corinthians 2:7-9)
- The Bible is a book about Heaven and St Paul captured the essence of the Christian existence in a few words "For to me to live is Christ, and to die is gain." (Philippians 1:21-23)

- "The Lord is not slow about His promise, as some count slowness, but is patient toward you, not wishing for any to perish but for all to come to repentance." (2 Peter 3:9)

CAN A PERSON BE SURE OF GOING TO HEAVEN?

Perhaps this was the most revealing question I asked my interviewees in preparation for this book. By their answers I came to learn that most were not sure.

The Other Italians answered the question by quoting the Bible or paraphrasing the scriptures. Most explained it with these or similar words which indicate the need for a person to have a relationship with Jesus:

<u>Sin separates a person from God</u> - "For the wages of sin is death; but the gift of God is eternal life through Jesus Christ our Lord." (Romans 6:23)

<u>Recognize God has a plan for you</u> - "I am come that they might have life and have it abundantly." (John 10:10)

<u>God sent His son Jesus to die for your sins</u> - "God demonstrates His love toward us that while we were yet sinners, Christ died for us." (Romans 5:8)

Recognize that the best intentions of religion are void of the promises of God:

"Jesus answered and said, <u>I am the way</u> the truth and the life. No man cometh unto the Father but by me!" (John 14:6)

"For <u>by grace are ye saved through faith</u>; and that not of yourselves: it is the gift of God!" (Ephesians 2:8)

"If we confess our sins He is faithful and just to forgive us our sins and cleanse us from all unrighteousness." (I John 1:9)

Here is another descriptor offered by one of my interviewees during my questioning:

"Come clean — that you are a sinner and in need of a Savior." (Rom 6:23) "ALL have sinned and fall short of the glory of God."

"Get rid of your human and religious ideas - read and believe the Bible. Lose the idea that you can or must do something to inherit eternal life. (Acts 16:31): "Believe on the Lord Jesus Christ and thou shall be saved.""

"Acknowledge that you can do nothing to earn God's forgiveness. (John 3:16): "For God so loved the world that HE gave his only begotten Son that whosoever believes on Him shall not perish but have everlasting life.""

"Accept Jesus Christ as your Lord and Savior: (Acts 4:12) "Nor is there salvation in any other, for there is no other name under heaven given among men by which we must be saved.""

The Other Italians believe if a person desires to go to heaven they must get into that relationship with the Savior.

A person's religion cannot substitute for an intimate and personal relationship with Jesus Christ. An individual does this by a confession of their sinful condition, and a declaration to make Him the controlling force in your life.

St. John, known as the beloved Disciple, quoted the words of Jesus when He explained the "way to heaven" to a Jewish leader named, Nicodemus: "For God loved the world so much that he gave his only Son so that anyone who believes in him shall not perish but have eternal life."

Chapter Twenty:
Absolution or Absolute Forgiveness?

Absolution in the Roman Catholic Church is the act of being forgiven through the Sacrament of Penance. Throughout its history, the Church has convened various councils to refine and revise certain theological positions in various areas of Church administration. The Council of Trent (1545 – 1563) defined the issue of penance: "As a means of regaining grace and justice, penance was at all times necessary for those who had defiled their souls with any mortal sin... Before the coming of Christ, penance was not a sacrament, nor is it since His coming a sacrament for those who are not baptized. But the Lord then principally instituted the Sacrament of Penance, when, being raised from the dead, he breathed upon His disciples saying: 'Receive ye the Holy Ghost. Whose sins you shall forgive, they are forgiven them; and whose sins you shall retain, they are retained.' (John 20:22-23) By which action so signal and words so clear the consent of all the Fathers has ever understood that the power of forgiving and retaining sins was communicated to the Apostles and to their lawful successors, for the reconciling of the faithful who have fallen after Baptism. (Sess.XIVc. i)

Later on the council expressly states that Christ left priests, His own vicars, as judges (praesides et judices), unto whom all the mortal crimes into which the faithful may have fallen should be revealed in order that, in accordance with the power of the keys, they may pronounce the sentence of forgiveness or retention of sins." (Sess. XIV, c. v)

The Other Italians cannot find any scriptures where Jesus instituted the "Sacrament of Penance!" Nowhere in the scriptures did Christ appoint "his own vicars as judges or priests;" nor did he gave anyone authority to "forgive sins."

As for giving the disciples the "authority to forgive sins, there appears to be a scripture that the Church uses to justify this sacrament, but when the historic language is translated on the basis of the full background of the ministry of Jesus, and His teaching, the meaning bears no footing for any mortal to forgive the sins of another. As for the scripture that records the conversation Jesus had with His disciples, theologians agree that it does not give Disciples the authority or power to forgive or not forgive someone of their sins, but the ability to discern! "If you forgive the sins of any, their sins have been forgiven them; if you retain the sins of any, they have been retained. " John 20:23

Now, reading the passage, one could get the idea that the Disciples were indeed given some extraordinary power to "forgive a persons sin...or not forgive them." To fully understand the meaning of this scripture is to follow the same rules theologians and Bible scholars follow; look at the context of the entire Bible, the context of the book, examine the chapter, and work back from the verse in question.

Did Jesus give the Disciples some extra power to actually forgive sins? The Other Italians use the above schema that follows an accepted investigative protocol for scriptural study.

Throughout the Biblical one will read that only God can forgive sins. It is the consistent message from cover to cover! Mankind's sin is affront to God, and an individual must deal with Him for forgiveness. The Other Italians explain it thus: If we wrong someone, we don't go to a third party to appeal for our forgiveness. Ultimately, even if we send someone to "intercede for us," sooner or later we'll have to go to the individual with our apology."

Among the Israelites population were High Priests who offered a large-scale sacrifice for the sin of all the people in the form of an unspotted lamb. The lamb would be offered on an altar. This sacrifice was done every day. But at no time did the priests ever receive the power or ability to forgive sins.

When the Lord died on the Cross of Calvary, He represented that perfect lamb required by God because of His sinless life. Consider the words of John the Baptizer when he saw Jesus coming in to the waters where he was preaching. "The next day he saw Jesus coming to him and said, "Behold, the Lamb of God who takes away the sin of the world!" (St John 1:29)

The message of St. Peter clarifies the sacrifice: "For you know that it was not with perishable things such as silver or gold that you were redeemed from the empty way of life handed down to you from your forefathers, but with the precious blood of Christ, a lamb without blemish or defect. He was chosen before the creation of the world, but was revealed in these last times for your sake. Through him you believe in God, who raised him from the dead and glorified him, and so your faith and hope are in God."

The death of Jesus Christ finalized the debt the Priests only symbolically offered on behalf of the nation of Israel. The Other Italians question: "Why would any intercessor be necessary to offer payment for the sins of an individual or believe God's saving grace could be made manifest in anything other than the finished work of the Cross?"

It is fully understood by these Other Italians that Jesus does not need a representative, emissary, and intermediary to bestow his grace. As for the opening sentence where the Council of Trent uses the words "regaining grace," The Other Italians know that God's grace is endless, knows no bounds, and when the individual experiences the New Birth, His grace continues to flow in and through them. It is not extracted, doesn't need to be renewed and requires nothing to facilitate its divine power. The Bible record is explicit in that it states God's grace cannot be earned, merited, bought, sold, bartered or in any way achieved outside of it being a gift presented to the individual via the "sacrificial death of Jesus!"

THE CHARACTERISTICS OF GOD'S GRACE

The Other Italians believe:

- God's grace shows two main truths: His nature to be merciful, loving and forgiving, and the decadence of mankind-sinful! The action of God's grace shows us that he is the creator and we his creation.
- God's grace cannot in any other way be bestowed on the person except through the finished work of the cross. One doesn't go daily for a "dose," and walk away until he needs another dose. The scripture says; "My grace is sufficient for you, for my power is perfected in weakness." It is sufficient in that it is endless, comprehensive and powerful to keep the person.

No matter what we think we can give in exchange, it would be an insult to God who sacrificed His son to enjoin himself to his creation. The message of the scriptures proclaims there is absolutely nothing mankind can do to gain God's grace. If our accomplishments could earn God's grace it would no longer be "grace," but payment for being good. Consider the words of the prophet Isaiah:

"For all of us have become like one who is unclean, And all our righteous deeds are like a filthy garment; And all of us wither like a leaf, And our iniquities, like the wind, take us away." (Isaiah 64:6)

That's pretty strong language! In God's sight all of things we think make us righteous are abhorrence to Him. It is an offense to God to think we can bring Him something worthy of His grace.

God's grace bestowed on an individual produces a life of service to Him and others. The Other Italians understand God's grace is not a license to sin…but to serve. They will tell you that one has to spend his or her life in Christ-like living.

The noted theologian Charles Ryrie presents us with the following, "The final cause of the revelation of the grace of God in Christ is not creed, but character."

And consider the words of the Apostle Paul to Titus:

"For the grace of God has appeared, bringing salvation to all men," instructing us to deny ungodliness and worldly desires and to live sensibly, righteously and godly in the present age," (Titus 2:11)

The Other Italians believe God's grace comes with a guarantee: "God absolutely pledges to the individual continuous forgiveness." They do not question their salvation because it came with a assurance…never to wear out, be deleted, exchanged for some new promise, become defensible, withdrawn or someday need to be revised. Their salvation depends on God's continuous love and commitment, and not on anything they can do!

The Apostle Paul's letter to the Romans sums it: Who will bring a charge against God's elect? God is the one who justifies; who is the one who condemns? Christ Jesus is He who died, yes, rather who was raised, who is at the right hand of God, who also intercedes for us. Who will separate us from the love of Christ? Will tribulation, or distress, or persecution, or famine, or nakedness, or peril, or sword? Just as it is written, "For Your sake we are being put to death all day long; We were considered as sheep to be slaughtered. But in all these things we overwhelmingly conquer through Him who loved us. For I am convinced that neither death, nor life, nor angels, nor principalities, nor things present, nor things to come, nor powers, nor height, nor depth, nor any other created thing, will be able to separate us from the love of God, which is in Christ Jesus our Lord. (Romans 8:33-39)

The Other Italians have a continuous reliance on the Bible for their daily living and believe God's grace is seen in their every day life! The idea of being a conqueror shows the Christian life is one of victory, not defeat! They hear the message of St. Paul's letter to the Church in Rome: "But in all these things we overwhelmingly conquer through Him who loved us!" Romans 8:37

The Other Italians believe Jesus died once and for all people. They maintain their belief in the scriptures that there is no other way to receive forgiveness for sin:

"For if you forgive men when they sin against you, <u>your heavenly Father will also forgive you.</u> But if you do not forgive men their sins, your Father will not forgive your sins." (Matthew 6:14-15)

If we confess our sins, <u>He is faithful and just and will forgive us</u> our sins and purify us from all unrighteousness." (1 John 1:9)

"I, even <u>I, am he who blots out your transgressions</u>, for my own sake, and remembers your sins no more. Review the past for me, let us argue the matter together; state the case for your innocence." (Isaiah 43:25-26)

"Repent, then, and <u>turn to God, so that your sins may be wiped out</u>, that times of refreshing may come from the Lord," (Acts 3:19)

"Come now, let us reason together," says the LORD. "Though your sins are like scarlet, they shall be as white as snow; though they are red as crimson, they shall be like wool." (Isaiah 1:18)

"Therefore, if anyone is in Christ, he is a new creation; the old has gone, the new has come!" (2 Corinthians 5:17)

"In Him we have redemption through his blood, the forgiveness of sins, in accordance with the riches of God's grace." (Ephesians 1:7)

"Their sins and lawless acts <u>I will remember no more.</u>" (Hebrews 10:17)

"The Lord our God is merciful and forgiving, even though we have rebelled against him;" (Daniel 9:9)

"<u>For he has rescued us from the dominion of darkness</u> and brought us into the kingdom of the Son he loves, in whom we have redemption, the forgiveness of sins. (Colossians 1:13-14)

"…as far as the east is from the west, so far has <u>He removed our transgressions</u> from us." (Psalm 103:12)

"In accordance with your great love, forgive the sin of these people, just as you have pardoned them from the time they left Egypt until now." The LORD replied, "I have forgiven them, as you asked. Nevertheless, as surely as I live and as surely as the glory of the LORD fills the whole earth." (Numbers 14:19-21)

"Who is a God like you, who pardons sin and forgives the transgression of the remnant of his inheritance? You do not stay angry forever but delight to show mercy. You will again have compassion on us; you will tread our sins underfoot and hurl all our iniquities into the depths of the sea." (Micah 7:18-19

"This, then, is how you should pray:" 'Our Father in heaven, hallowed be your name, your kingdom come, your will be done on earth as it is in heaven. Give us today our daily bread. Forgive us our debts, as we also have forgiven our debtors. And lead us not into temptation, but deliver us from the evil one. For if you forgive men when they sin against you, your heavenly Father will also forgive you. But if you do not forgive men their sins, your Father will not forgive your sins." (Matthew6:9-15) ("Debts" means our failures)

"And when you stand praying, if you hold anything against anyone, forgive him, so that your Father in heaven may forgive you your sins." (Mark 11:25)

"for this is My blood of the covenant, which is poured out for many for forgiveness of sins." (Matthew 26:28)

Catholic Canon Law is comprised of hundreds of rules, clauses, exceptions, rites, regulations and edicts governing the "confessions" of the individual and groups. The Church offers 'absolution' for their sins as "intermediary between man and God."

It is not the argument of The Other Italians to contest these practices on any personal inclination or idea independent of what the BIBLE says. That is the only source of their belief; that Jesus died once and for all, that His blood and only His blood cleanses the individual of his or her sin, that His grace is sufficient to save and preserve their salvation, and that Jesus is the only advocate and intermediary for them and they confess their sins to God in His.

They hold to the scriptures that address this issue: "He saved us, not on the basis of deeds which we have done in righteousness, but according to His mercy, by the washing of regeneration and renewing by the Holy Spirit," (Titus 3:5)

"This is the message we have heard from Him and announce to you, that God is Light, and in Him there is no darkness at all. If we say that we have fellowship with Him and yet walk in the darkness, we lie and do not practice the truth; but if we walk in the Light as He Himself is in the Light, we have fellowship with one another, and the blood of Jesus His Son cleanses us from all sin. If we say that we have no sin, we are deceiving ourselves and the truth is not in us. If we confess our sins, He is faithful and righteous to forgive us our sins and to cleanse us from all unrighteousness. If we say that we have not sinned, we make Him a liar and His word is not in us." (1 John 1:5-10)

"We have a great high priest who has passed through the heavens, Jesus the Son of God, let us hold fast our confession. For we do not have a high priest who cannot sympathize with our weaknesses, but One who has been tempted in all things as we are, yet without sin. Therefore let us draw near with confidence to the throne of grace, so that we may receive mercy and find grace to help in time of need." (Hebrews 4:4-16)

The Roman Catholic Church's believes it can offer forgiveness of sins through confession and absolution because it assumes Christ and the Church are ONE!

This is the basis of the irreconcilable differences!

According to the Catholic Catechism, the Church can forgive sins in the name of Jesus Christ! It also dictates what must be done to receive forgiveness in the order of praying, "Hail Mary's" and "Our Fathers."

Noted theologian, Richard Phillips (Master of Divinity -Westminster Theological Seminary) writes:

"The Bible says, "There is one mediator between God and man, the man Christ Jesus" (1 Tim. 2:5) "Jesus remains head of his church, and he has not delegated this headship to the pope or any other person. Therefore, we must confess our sins to God through Christ. We need not perform any acts of penance, but only offer up sincere repentance and faith in Christ's blood. 1 John 1:9 tells us to confess our sins to him: "If we confess our sins, he Jesus is faithful and just to forgive us our sins and to cleanse us from all unrighteousness" (1 Jn. 1:9). Any sacramental system of confession – including Rome's – that would have us appeal to anyone other than Jesus and to seek any other satisfaction than his finished work on the cross is an abomination to God that perverts the gospel and leaves the sinner in bondage not merely to his or her sins but to the Church as well.

Chapter Twenty-One:
The Sacrament of Holy Orders

The basic doctrines of the Roman Catholic Church include seven sacraments, while The Other Italians celebrate only two: baptism and communion...those that were established by Jesus through example. The divide is seen in sacraments that are said to bestow God's grace on the individual.

One such sacrament is that of "Holy Orders" where there is the establishment of ordination for church leaders: Bishop, Priest, and Deacon. Each level of ordination bestows special graces: the ability to preach, (given to deacons). It also grants the ability to act in the person of Christ to offer the Mass.

Here again The Other Italians hold to the scriptures that do not elevate anyone to the position of mediator, interceder, or any superior position within the body of Christ. They acknowledge there are different ministries, but they site that nowhere in the Bible is any extra ability or divine power given to mankind to execute the forgiveness of sins or act in the place of the Lord Jesus.

The manifest of the Bible proclaims that when an individual approaches God in the name of Jesus, is repentant of their sins and asks for forgiveness, it is granted (Only God can determine the mind and heart of the individual in this action). As written in the previous chapters, He never conferred any power to His disciples or anyone else to forgive anyone's sin nor is there any record in the New Testament that they ever attempted to forgive anyone's sin. They certainly had the ability to discern those who were demon possessed and those spouting counterfeit doctrines. They were to oversee, instruct and help the early churches to identify sin and doctrinal error and its destructive force within the congregations.

The Apostle Paul, the writer of most of the New Testament, said he preached, Christ and Christ crucified. The focus of Christianity is the cross…the death of Jesus for the sins mankind. Doctrines that add and subtract from the completed work of the Cross are considered "bogus."

As for their "duties," Jesus was daily preparing the Disciples for ministry to people. He empowered them with insight into motives, but never gave them power to forgive sins.

In the book of St. John 20:23 we read the following interaction with the Disciples: "Again Jesus said, 'Peace be with you! As the Father has sent me, I am sending you.' And with that he breathed on them and said, "Receive the Holy Spirit!'"

He commanded them to go out and bring the good news of salvation to the world. Jesus was physically leaving the earth, but promised God would be with them in the person of the Holy Spirit living in them.

Without Jesus by their side, the Disciples would need the ability to proclaim the Good News with the same boldness and confidence He had shone during the three years of his ministry. With assurance, the Disciples would be able to confidently tell individuals that if they truly believed the message, their sins would absolutely be forgiven. On the other hand, they would also be able to avow that if they didn't believe the message, they were not forgiven. By reason of anything they did or believed in substitution for the message of faith, brought condemnation on them. Of course, God would be the ultimate judge of the intentions of their heart.

The difference between the first Disciples and those who follow Jesus today is that for them the scriptures had not yet been given. They needed that special insight (or what is know to some theologians as "spiritual anointing") into the motives of those to whom they shared the "good news."

Today, the Christian can rely on the scriptures for wisdom and discernment: "All Scripture is inspired by God and profitable for teaching, for reproof, for correction, for training in righteousness; (2 Timothy 3:16)

<u>In summation of this issue, the disciples were given the power to spiritually discern the condition of men and women - but not the power to forgive sins</u>.

Typically, the "Other Italian" is not a Bible scholar, although they are students of the scriptures! What he or she does have is a reliance on the Holy Spirit to clarify the message of the scriptures. While most individuals in the Christian community know the "stories" within the Bible, many may not understand the meaning of them nor have they applied the "lessons" within each to their lives.

For some people the idea of reading the Bible is met with anxiety because they have not been encouraged to do so as part of the walk with Christ. The key to understanding them is one's reliance on the Holy Spirit, which Jesus promised, "would lead them into all truth!"

The Other Italians understand the Bible is complete! What they find therein is a path to discipleship whereby they daily yield their lives to the Lord Jesus, and grow spiritually…that is to say, have a "disciplined life," which is focused on their relationship with God through Him. No substitute or representative of the clergy is necessary! This remains an irreconcilable difference!

The Catechism of the Roman Catholic Church, article 1549 reads: "Through the ordained ministry, especially that of bishops and priests, the presence of Christ as head of the Church is made visible in the midst of the community of believers. In the beautiful expression of St. Ignatius of Antioch, the bishop is typos tou Patros: he is like the living image of God the Father."

The Other Italians do not accept the premise of a substitutionary Christ in their lives because the Bible is clear in the matter of who can be "like the image of God the Father!" They are aware of the presence of God on earth and refer to the scriptures for guidance in this matter should someone claim to be a reflection or representation of God.

It is found in Colossians 1:15-16: "For He rescued us from the domain of darkness, and transferred us to the kingdom of His beloved Son, in whom we have redemption, the forgiveness of sins. He is the image of the invisible God, the firstborn of all creation. For by Him all things were created, both in the heavens and on earth, visible and invisible, whether thrones or dominions or rulers or authorities all things have been created through Him and for Him. He is before all things, and in Him all things hold together."

Jesus, and only Jesus is the image of God! He proclaimed, "I and the Father are one." (John 10:30) That word one doesn't only mean they agree with each other; it is more than that. They are of one spirit or nature! The truth is - only "God" can be of the same nature as "God!" Jesus declared who He is to a Disciple: "Philip said to Him, 'Lord, show us the Father, and it is enough for us.' Jesus said to him, 'Have I been so long with you, and yet you have not come to know Me, Philip? He who has seen Me has seen the Father; how can you say, 'Show us the Father'? Do you not believe that I am in the Father, and the Father is in Me? The words that I say to you I do not speak on My own initiative, but the Father abiding in Me does His works.'" (John 14:8-10)

Mankind has not seen God in His heavenly form and glory; but we have seen His image in Jesus (not in the physical body of Jesus but rather in His actions and teachings…in His nature…in his Word).

The affidavit of the scriptures declares: "For it was the Father's good pleasure for all the fullness to dwell in Him" (Colossians 1:19). All the fullness of Deity dwelt in Jesus, who declared: "For I have come down from heaven, not to do My own will, but the will of Him who sent Me." (John 6:38)

Finally, few of my interviewees knew the promise which is found in 2 Corinthians 5:21 - "He made Him (Jesus) who knew no sin to be sin on our behalf, so that we might become the righteousness of God in Him."

The Other Italians are excited to share their faith. According to them, they have experienced a spiritual re-birth, and it has brought about "incredible things" in their lives. They are not perfect by any means…what they say they are…is "forgiven."

They believe the Bible confirms what they are experiencing: "Therefore having such a hope, we use great boldness in our speech, and are not like Moses, who used to put a veil over his face so that the sons of Israel would not look intently at the end of what was fading away. But their minds were hardened; for until this very day at the reading of the old covenant the same veil remains unlifted, because it is removed in Christ. But to this day whenever Moses is read, a veil lies over their heart; but whenever a person turns to the Lord, the veil is taken away. Now the Lord is the Spirit, and where the Spirit of the Lord is, there is liberty. But we all, with unveiled face, beholding as in a mirror the glory of the Lord, are being transformed into the same image from glory to glory, just as from the Lord, the Spirit. (2 Corinthians 3:12-18) That image is not that one becomes invisible, but that he or she learns the mind Christ through the scriptures! Here is the promise found in therein: Therefore if anyone is in Christ he is a new creature; the old things passed away; behold, new things have come." Here it is in the Living Bible: "When someone becomes a Christian, he becomes a brand new person inside. He is not the same anymore. A new life has begun!" (2 Corinthians 5:17)

The Other Italians did not say this...the Bible does!

Chapter Twenty-Two:
Last Rites – Purgatory – Prayer for the dead

In Roman Catholicism there is what is known as the Last Rites, Purgatory and Prayer for the Dead. The Other Italians revert to the scriptures in the discussion of these beliefs.

LAST RITES

When I questioned members of the Roman Catholic Church about the future of a person not given the last rites upon death, most did not know for sure what happens. The Last Rites are not a singular sacrament but a combination of several: Penance, communion, and anointing the sick.

- First, it is not a requirement of the Church.
- Second, as mentioned it is an administration of several sacraments.
- Third, it does provide a means of grace in the hour of death according to Church doctrine.

The Other Italians cling to their faith that secures their salvation and eternal life through the acceptance of Jesus as the Lord in life and death. They don't believe you can add anything to the "finished work of the cross." It is a registered "Patent" in the vaults of Heaven. But the Church has indeed added things to the finished work of the cross!

PURGATORY

During the 16th century, the doctrine of Purgatory (a temporary state of post earth life) was adopted by the Church; however it has its historical roots hundreds of years before. It evolved out of Medieval Christian Theology and Philosophy, and was greatly influenced literary work of Dante Alighieri, who penned, "The Divine Comedy." His allegorical or symbolic vision of the afterlife was a strong influence in the adoption of this idea within the Roman Catholic Church. However, it has no Biblical authentication.

The Church defines Purgatory as "a state of final purification after death and before entrance into heaven for those who died in God's friendship, but were only imperfectly purified; a final cleansing of human imperfection before one is able to enter the joy of heaven." (Catechism of the Catholic Church [CCC] Page 896) The logic, or theological argument behind, what is identified as an intermediary state where the dead go, came from literature published in the writings of Fathers, Tertullian, Origen, Cyprian, Lactantius, Eusebius, Cyril, Gregory of Nyssa, Epiphanius, Jerome, Ambrose, John Chrysostom, Augustine, Gregory the Great, Venerable Bede and second millennium theologians such as Anselm, Bernard, Aquinas and Bonaventure, that alleges there is a "way station" where a person actually goes before finding a final destination in either heaven or hell.

The reasoning for a place called Purgatory was initially centered on the issue of prayers for the dead. The idea of praying for the dead reaches far back in history with the earliest pagan cultures. Again, we're reminded of the civilizations that sought some kind of "spiritual enlightenment," and created worship practices based on man's idea of an almighty...or 'almighties!' (Permit me)

As the Roman Catholic Church adopted the practice, controversial issues surrounding it rose as some Church leaders and theologians argued it was not a practice of the New Testament Church and there was no evidence in the scriptures to even inferentially support it.

Such prayers for the departed only made sense if there was some other realm where the dead could go prior to their acceptance into heaven or ultimately be damned with an eternal existence in hell. Key to this discussion is this: The defenders argued that if the person who died and was already in Heaven, prayers would be meaningless; if he or she were in Hell, praying would be futile. Logic outweighed the Holy Scriptures!

But The Other Italians again revert to the scriptures to answer the questions circling a proposed intermediary place for members to go upon their death. They base their view, not on historical literature, the views of theologians or books that are not accepted as part of canon of scriptures from which we get our present Bible. The Roman Catholic view of Purgatory finds its roots in what is known as the Apocrypha (Twelve "un-authenticated" additional books that sometimes appear in some Bible publications).

Today, these do not appear in the canon of scriptures for many reasons, among them are:

- None of the books is written in the Hebrew Language.
- Not one of the writers lay claim to have been "inspired" to write their book.
- It was not until 1546 that the Roman Catholic Church "canonized" these books because they supported the idea of Purgatory, praying for the dead and other characteristics of worship. This is direct opposition to the texts in the Bible that deal with death, afterlife and communication with or for the dead.
- It teaches immoral practices, such as lying, suicide, assassination and magical incantation.
- Throughout history, Jerome and other Roman Catholic scholars have rejected the Books of the Apocrypha because they were not consistent with the sixty-six books that were consistent in message and have attained credible authenticity.

The Other Italians reject this intermediate state held to be true by the Roman Catholic Church, and subscribe to a scriptural base for the after-life of an individual as shown in the epistle to the Hebrews: "And as it is appointed unto men once to die, but after this the judgment;" (Hebrews 9:27)

They believe there is confusion when those seeking Gods plan for their lives, move or detour from the Bible. The idea of a Christian going to a place called, "Purgatory," places doubt in the mind of the parishioner as to whether he or she has any guarantee at all as to the saving grace of God. Either heaven it is what Jesus set forth in the Gospels, and was taught in the Epistles or the individual is left to rely on the interpretations and adaptation of Church dogma - that which it has accumulated through the centuries.

In my study of Purgatory I happened upon a most interesting editorial from the Lancaster, Pennsylvania news (Lancaster Intelligencer), and the subject is the after-life of Pope John Paul II. When I questioned members of the Roman Catholic Church as to where the Pope went upon his death, everyone stated that he was "taken right up to heaven!" Ironically, the Pope did not have this assurance.

The Pope was profound in his "last will and testament" when he wrote, "I do not know when the moment will come, but like everything else, I place it too in the hands of the Mother of my Master: Totus Tuus."

The words, Totus Tuus were this Pope's motto. It means, totally yours, and expressed his complete 'consecration' to Mary. Within the text of his last will and testament the Pope leaves the reader with doubts about his own eternal salvation and no assurance as to where he will spend eternity. This was news for some of those I interviewed within the Roman Catholic Church, who thought the "Vicar of God," ("One who acts in the place of Jesus on earth") would absolutely be certain where he was going upon his death. Whether one believes in the office of the Pope or not, this proved to be a frightening revelation about the prospects of going to heaven from the man who interprets the Bible for a billion people. The individual who submitted this editorial reflects on the same insecurity The Other Italians faced while they were members in the Roman Catholic Church. It is written in somewhat of a sarcastic tone, but reveals the heart and mind of the Pope:

"Editorial Submitted May 2005 by Jamie Mitchell (The Lancaster Intelligencer) "Nice Pope, But No Hope"

"Dear Editor: I don't want to stir up any "holy wars" or sound condemning of the catholic faith but watching all the coverage and reading all the stories about the Pope in the Intell has caused me to be troubled in my soul. As I have come to learn, the Pope is the

"Vicar of Christ" – this means he speaks for Christ, acts on His behalf and even makes confessions of the people's sin to Christ. I have been fascinated to learn that when the Pope sits on "Peter's seat" and speaks - he is speaking "ex-cathedra." This means he is sharing infallible words, inspired by God – so divine are those words that no Pope can change or contradict those words. The fact is he is the supreme leader of the largest denomination in the world and by its doctrine; he has a direct pipeline to God.

Here is my angst...How is it that there is no assurance of this man's eternal destiny? There is a belief that he will get to heaven at some point – but no absolute assurance? I was overwhelmed that the POPE needed to be administered the Last Rites, which I discovered on catholic.org, is a sacrament that attempts to help him re-establish his salvation because of sins he might of committed and pray for his healing by illnesses caused by sin." Attempts to re-establish his salvation?" Millions of Catholics have been called upon to pray for his soul in "hopes" that he will get to heaven. According to Catholic Doctrine, he is in purgatory awaiting his eminent ascension into heaven, yet no one knows when that will be. Crowds of people will light candles, purchase prayer cards and say the Rosary to assist him into his eternal rest. I am totally baffled?

Is that not disconcerting that the one person who has been the mediator between an entire Church and God has no hope of heaven upon his death? What does that mean for the common person? And why does that not trouble the millions of Catholics that after all their rituals, rites and religious devotion – at the time of death, have no hope for themselves and their Pope. Over the years I have met numbers of sincere and devout Catholics who morally, ethically and spiritually are "saints" and yet they have no hope, which is troubling and sad. I have personally appreciated this Pope's commitment to moral issues and politically speaking, he has done much to encourage freedom around the globe. Most of my adult life I have listened and watched his every move; he is receiving the honor due a great world leader. Yet it must cause anxiety to consider that your life is spent thinking about God and heaven and yet you don't have any guarantees to get there – even when you are the number one guy!"

PRAYER FOR THE DEAD

While The Other Italians mourn for their dead, they adhere to the scriptures that say praying for and to the dead are strictly forbidden. When the Children of Israel entered the Promised Land, God laid down some ground rules. Under no circumstances were they to adapt, acknowledge or blend in with the cult practices of the people dwelling there. They were to be set apart!

"When you enter the land which the Lord your God gives you, you shall not learn to imitate the detestable things of those nations. There shall not be found among you anyone who makes his son or his daughter pass through the fire (Moloch was the Sun God and the Israelites were told not to submit their children to the "fire" which in ceremony would sometimes consume them), one who uses divination, one who practices witchcraft, or one who interprets omens, or a sorcerer, or one who casts a spell, or a medium, or a spiritist, or one who calls up the dead. For whoever does these things is detestable to the Lord;" (Deuteronomy 18)

The Other Italians do not believe in praying for the dead because nowhere in the ministry of Jesus did he ever instruct anyone to do so. They believe praying for the dead is disobedience to the scriptures; but they accept the Biblical instruction that acceptance of Jesus as Savior and Lord is the only requirement for salvation, and cite the ministry of Jesus to people like Nicodemus (St. John 3:16): "For God so loved the world, that He gave His only begotten Son, that whoever believes in Him shall not perish, but have eternal life."

At the point of death an individual's eternal future is sealed. They are saved through faith through in Christ and are in God's presence or they are in hell.

St. Luke bears upon this message with an illustration: "And there was a certain beggar named Lazarus, which was laid at his gate, full of sores, "Now there was a rich man, and he habitually dressed in purple and fine linen, joyously living in splendor every day. And a poor man named Lazarus was laid at his gate, covered with sores, and longing to be fed with the crumbs which were falling from the rich man's table; besides, even the dogs were coming and licking his sores. Now the poor man died and was carried away by the angels to Abraham's bosom; and the rich man also died and was buried. In Hades he lifted up his eyes, being in torment, and saw Abraham far away and Lazarus in his bosom. And he cried out and said, 'Father Abraham, have mercy on me, and send Lazarus so that he may dip the tip of his finger in water and cool off my tongue, for I am in agony in this flame.' But Abraham said, 'Child, remember that during your life you received your good things, and likewise Lazarus bad things; but now he is being comforted here, and you are in agony. And besides all this, between us and you there is a great chasm fixed, so that those who wish to come over from here to you will not be able, and that none may cross over from there to us. And he said, 'Then I beg you, father, that you send him to my father's house—for I have five brothers—in order that he may warn them, so that they will not also come to this place of torment.' But Abraham said, 'They have Moses and the Prophets; let them hear them.' But he said, 'No, father Abraham, but if someone goes to them from the dead, they will repent!' But he said to him, 'If they do not listen to Moses and the Prophets, they will not be persuaded even if someone rises from the dead." (St. John 16:19-31)

St. Paul wrote in his second letter to the Church in Corinth… "to be absent from the body was to be at home and present with the Lord." (2 Corinthians 5:8) In another letter to the Church in Philippi he declared: "For to me, to live is Christ and to die is gain. Now if I am to go on living in the body, this will mean productive work for me; yet I don't know what I prefer: I feel torn between the two, because I have a desire to depart and be with Christ, which is better by far." (Philippians 1:21-23)

The Other Italians conclude the only possible basis for someone to believe they can pray for the dead is found in the book of Revelation (Revelation 6:10). There we read about saints (martyrs) who cry out to God to avenge their blood. Stop at the verse and there is an argument; but in the very next chapter, the martyred saints in heaven are seen in total rest.

THE LAST BLESSING

The Catholic Catechism contains information about the last blessing. It is a protocol for the anointing and prayer of the individual who is dying: "The anointing is ordinarily succeeded by the conferring of the Apostolic benediction, or "last blessing," as it is commonly called. To this blessing a plenary indulgence is attached, to be gained, however, only at the hour of death, i.e. it is given nunc pro tunc. It is conferred in virtue of a special faculty granted to the bishops and by them delegated quite generally to their priests. The conditions requisite for gaining it are the invocation of the Holy Name of Jesus at least mentally, acts of resignation by which the dying person professes his willingness to accept all his sufferings in reparation for his sins and submits himself entirely to the will of God."

Again, The Other Italians believe in their complete redemption through the death of Jesus. As for reaching heaven and having an individual or the Church mitigate the amount of suffering a Church member might receive in the hereafter, they have the assurance of the scriptures that promise: "Therefore there is now no condemnation for those who are in Christ Jesus!" (Romans 8:1). One woman I interviewed stated: "The Christian life is not one where you received God's grace one day and lose it the next. The Bible declares it is endless. If so, then why do people cling to teaching that is contrary?"

St. Paul declared: "But thanks be to God, who always leads us in triumph in Christ, and manifests through us the sweet aroma of the knowledge of Him in every place. For we are a fragrance of Christ to God among those who are being saved and among those who are perishing; to the one an aroma from death to death, to the other an aroma from life to life. And who is adequate for these things?" (2 Corinthians 2:14-16)

Here it is in the Living Bible: But thanks be to God! For through what Christ has done, he has triumphed over us so that now wherever we go he uses us to tell others about the Lord and to spread the Gospel like a sweet perfume. As far as God is concerned there is a sweet, wholesome fragrance in our lives. It is the fragrance of Christ within us, an aroma to both the saved and the unsaved all around us. To those who are not being saved, we seem a fearful smell of death and doom, while to those who know Christ we are a life-giving perfume

No one can arrive in heaven as a sinner because God cannot look at or be in the presence of sin; The Bible does not support the idea of a Purgatory or any intermediary location. The Other Italians trust the Word of God that declares He is preparing a "place for them" in heaven. It is not on the merit of their good deeds (These are beneficial to our neighbors and are an expectation of those who know Christ and proclaim Him), but because of the sacrificial death of Jesus. One does not stand before God hopeless and helpless if Christ is dwelling within them! Sin cannot enter heaven!

Here the complete and final decree as told to the Disciples and offered to every regenerated man or woman, "Do not let your heart be troubled; believe in God, believe also in Me. In My Father's house are many dwelling places; if it were not so, I would have told you; for I go to prepare a place for you. If I go and prepare a place for you, I will come again and receive you to Myself, that where I am, there you may be also. And you know the way where I am going." Thomas said to Him, "Lord, we do not know where You are going, how do we know the way?" Jesus said to him, "I am the way, and the truth, and the life; no one comes to the Father but through Me."

The Other Italians believe the message of the Gospel! There is assurance of salvation and a final "living place" in heaven for those who are in Christ!

Chapter Twenty-Three:
The Pope – Infallible?

John Mark was a Disciple of Christ and the author of the same Gospel bearing the name, "The Gospel of St. Mark." St. Mark (the name by which we have to come to know him) was defensive of the message of Jesus and wrote about his concerns for those who would take away, add, alter or lessen its authenticity.

Consider the testament of the Lord as recorded by Mark: "This people honors Me with their lips, But their heart is far away from Me. 'But in vain do they worship Me, Teaching as doctrines the precepts of men.' Neglecting the commandment of God, you hold to the tradition of men. He was also saying to them, 'You are experts at setting aside the commandment of God in order to keep your tradition." (Mark 15:8-9)

A closer look at these words, reveal his concern! In essence, he was identifying those people who wish to exchange the divine mind for the mind of man in defense of their traditions. "For who among men knows the thoughts of a man except the spirit of the man which is in him? Even so the thoughts of God no one knows except the Spirit of God. Now we have received, not the spirit of the world, but the Spirit who is from God, so that we may know the things freely given to us by God, which things we also speak, not in words taught by human wisdom, but in those taught by the

Spirit, combining spiritual thoughts with spiritual words." (1 Corinthians 2:11-13

The Other Italians are aware that other Christian religions today have, in part, evolved through the "mind of man." Some will argue that this is "divine revelation" – that they have the mind of Christ in these matters. The Other Italians site St. Paul's letter to the Church in Corinth (I Corinthians 2:1-16 LB) "Dear brothers, even when I first came to you I didn't use lofty words and brilliant ideas to tell you God's message. For I decided that I would speak only of Jesus Christ and his death on the cross. I came to you in weakness—timid and trembling. And my preaching was very plain, not with a lot of oratory and human wisdom, but the Holy Spirit's power was in my words, proving to those who heard them that the message was from God. I did this because I wanted your faith to stand firmly upon God, not on man's great ideas.

Yet when I am among mature Christians I do speak with words of great wisdom, but not the kind that comes from here on earth, and not the kind that appeals to the great men of this world, who are doomed to fall. Our words are wise because they are from God, telling of God's wise plan to bring us into the glories of heaven. This plan was hidden in former times, though it was made for our benefit before the world began. But the great men of the world have not understood it; if they had, they never would have crucified the Lord of Glory.

That is what is meant by the Scriptures which say that no mere man has ever seen, heard, or even imagined what wonderful things God has ready for those who love the Lord. But we know about these things because God has sent his Spirit to tell us, and his Spirit searches out and shows us all of God's deepest secrets. No one can really know what anyone else is thinking or what he is really like except that person himself. And no one can know God's thoughts except God's own Spirit. And God has actually given us his Spirit (not the world's spirit) to tell us about the wonderful free gifts of grace and blessing that God has given us. In telling you about these gifts we have even used the very words given to us by the Holy Spirit, not words that we as men might choose. So we use the Holy Spirit's words to explain the Holy Spirit's facts. But the man who isn't a Christian can't understand and can't accept these thoughts from God, which the Holy Spirit teaches us. They sound foolish to him because only those who have the Holy Spirit within them can understand what the Holy Spirit means. Others just can't take it in. But the spiritual man has insight into everything, and that bothers and baffles the man of the world, who can't understand him at all. How could he? For certainly he has never been one to know the Lord's thoughts or to discuss them with him, or to move the hands of God by prayer. But, strange as it seems, we Christians actually do have within us a portion of the very thoughts and mind of Christ."

The great conflict arises when the individual believes "sacred" customs are in the same divine realm as the scriptures. There is a difference and Jesus warned against those who would go astray from the scriptures: "Why do you yourselves transgress the commandment of God for the sake of your tradition?" (Matthew 15:3)

From their previous union, The Other Italians are aware the Church teaches the Pope has the authority to interpret the scriptures in such a way as to defend and justify its doctrine. Examples of this out-of-scripture dogma include: Mary's sinless state - she is the Queen of heaven - she ascended into heaven.

Historically, the great debates of the "Reformation," brought by Roman Catholic Priests, centered on the issue of Papal authority, the sale of indulgences, and that the Church had drifted away from Biblical teaching. The scriptures caution against any teaching that Christ is not the head of the Church, and that the scriptures are incomplete and flawed. These declarations can be found in the first to last books in the Bible. The fact that God is opposed to those who change or add to His Word is found in the book of Revelation and bear serious consequences: "and if anyone takes away from the words of the book of this prophecy, God will take away his part from the tree of life and from the holy city, which are written in this book."

BUT ISN"T THE POPE INFALLBILE?

Paragraph 100 of the Catholic Catechism reads as follows: "The task of interpreting the Word of God authentically has been entrusted solely to the

Magisterium of the Church, that is, to the Pope and to the bishops in communion with him."

- The Church teaches that the individual is not to interpret the scriptures. But the Psalmist counters: "The law of the LORD is perfect, converting the soul: the testimony of the LORD is sure, making wise the simple." (Psalm 19:7) The Other Italians find the message of the Bible is easy to read and understand. The mind and heart of the regenerated individual feeds on the clear teaching of the Word of God.
- Only the magisterium of the Church can interpret the scriptures. St. Peter, speaking to "ordinary, every day people," clarifies the position of the Christian in the Kingdom of God as one with authority: "But you (Those ordinary, every day people) are a chosen race, a royal priesthood, a holy nation, a people for God's own possession, so that you may proclaim the excellencies of Him who has called you out of darkness into His marvelous light;" (1 Peter 3:9)
- One needs theological training to read and understand the Bible. Jesus answers this with His assurance that He would send the Holy Spirit to lead the Christian into all truth: "I have many more things to say to you, but you cannot bear them now. But when He, the Spirit of truth, comes, He will guide you into all the truth; for He will not speak on His own initiative, but whatever He hears, He will speak; and He will disclose to you what is to come. He will glorify Me, for He will take of Mine and will disclose it to you."

HOW CAN THE OTHER ITALIANS CLAIM TO UNDERSTAND THE SCRIPTURES?

The ability to understand the Bible is based on the "spiritual condition" of the individual: "But a natural man does not accept the things of the Spirit of God, for they are foolishness to him; and he cannot understand them, because they are spiritually appraised. But he who is spiritual appraises all things, yet he himself is appraised by no one." (1 Corinthians 2:14-15)

Here it is in the Living Bible:

"But the man who isn't a Christian can't understand and can't accept these thoughts from God, which the Holy Spirit teaches us. They sound foolish to him because only those who have the Holy Spirit within them can understand what the Holy Spirit means. Others just can't take it in. But the spiritual man has insight into everything, and that bothers and baffles the man of the world, who can't understand him at all." (Living Bible)

The Catechism of the Roman Catholic Church decrees the Pope is the chief representative of Christ on Earth, and has the authority of the Lord Jesus Christ. The Other Italians can find no scriptural basis for this assumption. That the "interpretation of the scriptures has been given "solely," to him is a contradiction of the scriptures.

St. Peter and St. Paul's collective ministerial message to the New Testament Church was that the members be avid students of the Word of God. Their admonishment was to know the scriptures: "Be diligent to present yourself approved to God as a workman who does not need to be ashamed, accurately handling the word of truth." (2 Timothy 2:15) The inference of this scripture is to "know what the Word of God means" and apply it to one's life! It goes beyond the exercise of reading, and enters into the realms of understanding and application. Surely, both men would not have laid out an expectation that was impossible to attain or confirmed by the scriptures!

One would expect the idea of the Pope being infallible would be an irreconcilable difference, and it is! But questions evolve from those outside of this community. An article written by Rachel Donadio - published in The New York Times (2/17/13), confronts papal infallibility as the retirement of Pope Benedict poses fundamental questions regarding the issue:

- "In transforming an office with an aura of divinity into something far more human, Benedict's decision has sent shock waves through the Vatican hierarchy, who next month will elect his successor. But it has also puzzled the faithful and scholars, who wonder how a pope can be infallible one day and fallible again the next, and whether that might undermine the authority of church teaching."

Others comment:

- "What is the status of an ex-pope?" asked scholar, Kenneth Pennington, a professor of ecclesiastical and legal history at the Catholic University of America in Washington. "We have no rules about that at all. What is his title? What are his powers? Does he lose infallibility?"
- "Still, many remain puzzled by the larger implications. "From a theological point of view, how can a person be considered to be infallible and not be infallible anymore?"
- "That the supreme pontiff can pass authority to his successor at retirement rather than death inevitably introduces more ambiguity to the authority of church doctrine, some scholars say, since it calls into question the authority of the pontiff who promulgated that doctrine. "Benedict actually by resigning has introduced some cracks into that infallibility. It's bound to relativize doctrine," Diarmaid MacCulloch, professor of the history of the Church at Oxford University

WAS ST. PETER INFALLIBLE?

The Other Italians question the infallibility of St. Peter (Identified as the "First Pope," according to Roman Catholic teaching). The facts bear out that Peter was one of the three close friends of Jesus. (Mt. 17:1 - 26:36-37) He traveled a rocky road from the day he met Jesus to the time he was an Apostle to the New Testament Church. That said, it must be related that nowhere in the scriptures is he singled out as the "leader of the church" or given a title of supreme church leader and any title other than "Apostle." One would think the person to be the head of the Christian Church would bring stability and unwavering devotion to the Master. If he was truly a candidate to be the first "Pope" of The Roman Catholic Church, his credentials certainly are fragile:

Peter denied the Lord Jesus three times. (Mt. 26:69-75)

Peter was a married man: (1 Cor. 9:5-Matthew 8:14)

The Lord rebuked Peter: (Mt. 16:23)

Peter was rebuked by the Apostle Paul: (Galatians 2:11)

Peter never accepted any reverence: (Acts 10:25-26); (Rev. 19:10 - 22:9)

Peter was not superior to the other apostles: (Mt. 18:18; 2 Cor.11:5-12:11)

Peter and the other apostles, in consideration of their demise, wrote letters preserving their combined God-given revelations for all time: (2 Pet. 1:12-15; 3:1-2; Eph. 3:3-5)

Peter along with the other apostles were to "sit on twelve thrones, judging the twelve tribes of Israel." (Mt. 19:28)

Peter was not the head of the church -Jesus is the only head of His church: (Eph. 1:22-23 - Col.1:19)

Peter was not selected to be the Vicar of Christ on earth: (no references to any elevation in the entire Bible). Peter never talked about any "successors" to himself.

Peter and Paul never wore any of the many titles of the modern Popes: (Pontiff, Vicar, His Holiness, Holy Father) (2 Peter 3:15)

Peter and no other disciple(s) were to be "the greatest in the kingdom." (Mt. 18:1-4 - 20:20-28); rather, they were to be equal.

Peter's name in the Greek is "petros" (a detached stone, or a stone among man, (John. 1:42) but Jesus said the church would be built upon the "rock" or Petra (a mass of rock, a boulder): (Mt. 16:18)

Peter is masculine gender and rock in feminine gender; in context they cannot refer to the same thing. Peter, himself, declared that Jesus was "the chief cornerstone:" (Acts 4:12; Eph. 2:20).

Peter and the other apostles were merely the layers of the foundation Stone – Jesus: (Acts 4:11-12; Eph. 2:19-20).

Finally, Jesus Himself said that "all authority" was given to Him both "in heaven and on earth." (Mt. 28:18-20).

<u>There are warnings about changing the scriptures:</u>

"You shall not add to the word which I am commanding you, nor take away from it, that you may keep the commandments of the Lord your God which I command you." (Deuteronomy 4:2)

"Do not add to His words or He will reprove you, and you will be proved a liar." (Proverbs 30:6)

David wrote a Psalm to proclaim the integrity of the Word: "The entirety of Your word is truth!" (Psalms 119: 160) "Every word of God is pure; he is a shield to those who put their trust in Him." (Proverbs 30:5-6)

The Revelation St. John received when exiled to the Island of Patmos culminates with these words: "For I testify unto every man that hears the words of the prophecy of this Book, If any man shall add unto these things, God shall add unto him the plagues that are written in this Book: And if any man shall take away from the words of the Book of this prophecy, God shall take away his part out of the Book of Life, and out of the holy city, and from the things which are written in this Book!" (Revelation 22:18-19)

The Other Italians site there is no scriptural basis for "papal infallibility" or the office of the papacy. Yet, the Roman Catholic Church imposes severe charges with a "curse to hell" (Anathema), for those who reject the authority of the Pope. This applies to members within the Church, and those outside who reject his authority. But The Other Italians profess the reality of a fearless state the Christian can and should live in as a result of having Jesus in their lives.

St. Paul penned this to a young Christian man: "God has not given us a spirit of fear and timidity, but of power, love, and self-discipline." (2 Timothy 1:7)

To Mary, the Angel said: "Fear not!"

To the Christian St. John writes: "There is no fear in love; but perfect love casts out fear, because fear involves punishment, and the one who fears is not perfected in love." (1 John 4:18)

Isaiah proclaimed: "Do not fear, for I am with you. Do not anxiously look about you, for I am your God. I will strengthen you, surely I will help you, Surely, I will uphold you with My righteous right hand." (Isaiah 41:10)

The Psalmist testified: "In God I have put my trust, I shall not be afraid. What can man do to me?" (Psalm 56:11)

Nowhere in the Bible is any man or woman given the spiritual authority to literally cast a person into hell for not believing the edicts of the church. It was not given by Jesus or taught in the ministry of the Disciples and Apostles. The Roman Catholic Church believes it has the final authority to interpret the scriptures…to their exclusion, in part, at times, if it deems necessary to maintain its dogma; and that the magisterium or ruling authority of the Church, through apostolic succession is necessary to interpret the scriptures for its members.

The Other Italians base their beliefs solely on the scriptures. In his second letter to Timothy, St. Paul wrote: "and that from childhood you have known the sacred writings which are able to give you the wisdom that leads to salvation through faith which is in Christ Jesus." Here it is in the Living Bible: "You know how, when you were a small child, you were taught the holy Scriptures; and it is these that make you wise to accept God's salvation by trusting in Christ Jesus." (1 Timothy 1:5)

Guess who Timothy's teachers were…the individuals who interpreted and taught him the scriptures? His mother and grandmother! By what authority did they presume to be able to read the scriptures, interpret and teach from them? The answer! Didn't Jesus say the Holy Spirit would lead into all truth?

The Other Italians believe to know God is to know His Word. St. Paul told his young protégé, Timothy: "All Scripture is inspired by God…" The original Hebrew said it was "God breathed!" This is why they stress the necessity of prayer, reading the Bible and allowing the Holy Spirit within, to lead them "believer" into ALL truth!

These Other Italians have learned to apply what they read in the Holy Scriptures to their life. One interviewee put it this way: "You're on an Island! You have all the provisions to live and you have a Bible. There is no Sunday school teacher, no preacher, no priest, no rabbi and no Pope. It is then that the Bible becomes relative to you and believe it or not, Christ will reveal Himself to you!" Jesus dwelling within you is the key to understanding the scriptures!"

Another said: "If a person truly wants to know who Jesus is, and what he can be in his or her life, they must embrace His word, without fear or doubt!"

Finally, another offered: "The real challenge for The Other Italians and members of the Roman Catholic Church is to determine the truth, not by who said it, but by what is said in the Bible!"

Chapter Twenty Four:
"Something Old and Something New"

The text of this chapter was drawn from discussion with theologians within the community of The Other Italians.

To more acutely understand the differences between the Roman Catholic Church and The Other Italians - is to expound on what the scriptures call the Old Covenant and New Covenant. In its simplest terms, "covenant" is defined as a promise. The extended meaning poses a promise to do or not do something. It is a legal term, sometimes employed in the field of real estate whereby usage of land is restricted.

But it takes on a more significant meaning when we see the terms used in the Scriptures. In the Biblical sense, it as a promise from God to do something for His creation! We shall examine the terms of each type of covenant to draw conclusions as to their impact on the issues discussed herein in explanation of the beliefs of a population this author has named:

THE OLD COVENANT

The inference one gets when the word "old" appears is one of transition, that it has been replaced, and it has, by what is known as (you guessed it) A New Covenant. God gave both promises! One is confining and condemning, and the other, liberating.

WHAT ARE THE TERMS OF THE OLD COVENANT?

God created man in His own image…that of being a "spiritual creation."

God established laws to protect and preserve his creation. To obey them was life, happiness and fellowship in His presence. But man disobeyed the laws. He sinned and was cast out of the presence of God. <u>His spiritual self was dead</u>. He was dead in his sin - he died "spiritually." From that moment on he needed to be "reborn spiritually."

The regeneration of his spirit would be based on receiving forgiveness for his sin. But man in his "fallen state" could do nothing to appease God for his sin! He was incapable of communicating with God as He was holy and could not be in the presence of sin. Something had to remove this impediment. The only payment would be death. Man had to die. But God was not willing to do or permit this.

God makes a promise! He will send the ultimate sacrifice as atonement for the sin of man! But until that time, he would establish a "covenant" to secure man's forgiveness.

He then gave primary laws of life for man to follow in the form of Ten Commandments. At this time, because man was dead spiritually, the laws are given on tablets of stone for mankind to physically see and read. If man would obey them, then deliverance from the separation with his maker would come. His sin would be blotted out and forgotten. He would be forever forgiven for his sin.

But man was incapable of keeping them because his sin nature was to choose that which was contrary to that which was good and acceptable behavior according to the laws of God. The flesh overpowered the spirit within him…because it was not of a divine nature as it once had been.

To maintain this promise, God chooses a people to carry the law until such time as the "Redeemer," the one who would be the ultimate sacrifice would arrive and offer himself as that final sacrifice. He calls a man who, by faith, withdrew from the pagan rituals of his community. His name was Abraham. His seed, which would someday number the "sand of the earth," was chosen people to be custodians and followers the laws of God. The idea of them being a "chosen people" does not mean in any way they were superior to other races, but given the privilege of living out the laws of God for all nations to witness and follow.

But Abraham's see, like Adam, were incapable of keeping the commandments. God was explicit in His demand: Follow the law and life, disobey and perish! A simple yet demanding contract was in force!

MAN WAS INCAPABLE OF KEEPING THE LAW

To offer an appeasement until the ultimate "spotless lamb" would be offered, Priests were to offer a living, spotless lamb as a sacrifice to the God.

Throughout their history, Prophets and Kings arose who desired the people to know the Laws of God and keep them. Unknowingly, the Prophets wrote about the coming Deliverer...known as the Messiah!

These Prophets preached a powerful message that someday the Laws of God would <u>not</u> be transported to mankind on tablets, scrolls or through any kind of judicial system; but would be transcribed on the heart and mind. They did not know at the time to call it such, but they were announcing a NEW COVENANT between God and Man.

Jeremiah, the Prophet confirmed the message: "But this is the covenant which I will make with the house of Israel after those days," declares the LORD, "I will put My law within them and on their heart I will write it; and I will be their God, and they shall be My people."

BUT HOW DO YOU GET THE WORDS ON STONES INTO A PERSON'S HEART?

The coming of Jesus was the fulfillment of the Prophecies that foretold His arrival. He came, ministered, died and came forth from the grave. His ministry on earth was to reflect the spirit of God to all men and women. Upon His death, He looks at His followers and all the followers since and promises THE NEW COVENANT.

"But when He, the Spirit of truth, comes, He will guide you into all the truth; for He will not speak on His own initiative, but whatever He hears, He will speak; and He will disclose to you what is to come." (St. John 16:13)

The Other Italians know that their spirit has been "reborn," it has come alive and now they can commune with God.

Now, here's the wonder of it all! With the Old Covenant man was doomed to die because he was incapable of living according to the law. The Apostle Paul wrote (as recorded in this text), man was "dead in his sin." That's spiritual death! Only one individual has ever kept the law…Jesus.

IS MAN NOW CAPABLE OF KEEPING THE LAW?

No! So how can he be righteous if he can't keep it? Christ within Him keeps it; thus when God looks down on the spiritually "regenerated" man and woman, He does not see them…He sees His Son, Jesus!

The Other Italians finally got the "message;" it is Christ dwelling within them who fulfills the requirement of the Law. God's will and purpose for them is now written on their heart with the blood of Jesus at the end of the quill!

Chapter Twenty-Five:
Final thoughts

As I penned this book I was fully aware that my task was more of a transcriber than an author, garnering, sorting and summarizing the information herein from interviews with those I have represented as The Other Italians. I am not a theologian, nor do I imagine myself to be one.

Having dedicated thousands of hours of intense research studying their beliefs, questioning them on specific topics, and recording scriptures relating to the same, I have become quite familiar with their beliefs, the testimony of their faith in the Scriptures as a means of knowing God, and their theology. On these pages I have endeavored to capture the "mind" of The Other Italians!

While The Other Italians are affiliated with many different churches, the one factor that predominates their beliefs is a total reliance on the Scriptures. So, borrowing from many sources to bring focus and discipline to my writing, I committed my pen to present only what they said, what they believe according to the scriptures, what I heard in sermons representative of their teaching, and the testimony of those who were willing to interview with me about the various issues in this book.

When I asked several members of this community how I should conclude this transcription, it was suggested that I not borrow from their personal testimony but from the scriptures.

The book of Romans chapter six is a summary of what The Other Italians believe. It contains the words of St. Paul the Apostle:

"Well then, shall we keep on sinning so that God can keep on showing us more and more kindness and forgiveness? Of course not! Should we keep on sinning when we don't have to? For sin's power over us was broken when we became Christians and were baptized to become a part of Jesus Christ; through his death the power of your sinful nature was shattered. Your old sin-loving nature was buried with him by baptism when he died; and when God the Father, with glorious power, brought him back to life again, you were given his wonderful new life to enjoy. For you have become a part of him, and so you died with him, so to speak, when he died; and now you share his new life and shall rise as he did. Your old evil desires were nailed to the cross with him; that part of you that loves to sin was crushed and fatally wounded, so that your sin-loving body is no longer under sin's control, no longer needs to be a slave to sin; for when you are deadened to sin you are freed from all its allure and its power over you. And since your old sin-loving nature "died" with Christ, we know that you will share his new life. Christ rose from the dead and will never die again. Death no longer has any power over him. He died once for all to end sin's power, but now he lives forever in unbroken fellowship with God. So look upon your old sin nature as dead and unresponsive to sin, and instead be alive to God, alert to him, through Jesus Christ our Lord. Do not let sin control your puny body any longer; do not give in to its sinful desires. Do not let any part of your bodies become tools of wickedness, to be used for sinning; but give yourselves completely to God—every part of you—for you are back from death and you want to be tools in the hands of God, to be used for his good purposes. Sin need never again be your master, for now you are no longer tied to the law where sin enslaves you, but you are free under God's favor and mercy. Does this mean that now we can go ahead and sin and not worry about it? (For our salvation does not depend on keeping the law but on receiving God's grace!) Of course not! Don't you realize that you can choose your own master? You can choose sin (with death) or else obedience (with acquittal). The one to whom you offer yourself—he will take you and be your master, and you will be his slave. Thank God that though you once chose to be slaves of sin, now you have obeyed with all your heart the teaching to which God has committed you. And now you are free from your old master, sin; and you have become slaves to your new master, righteousness. I speak this way, using the illustration of slaves and masters, because it is easy to understand: just as you used to be slaves to all kinds of sin, so now you must let yourselves be slaves to all that is right and holy. In those days when you were slaves of sin you didn't bother much with goodness. And what was the result? Evidently not good, since you are ashamed now even to think about those things you used to do, for all of them end in eternal doom. But now you are free from the power of sin and are slaves of God, and his benefits to you include holiness and everlasting life. For the wages of sin is death, but the free gift of God is eternal life through Jesus Christ our Lord."(LB)

So this ends my task! I place no errand for the reader to agree or disagree with what has been stated herein, but have the assurance I have faithfully and accurately presented what this population of The Other Italians believe and why!

Other Books by David Mercaldo, PhD

David Mercaldo's books can be ordered from Amazon.com or ask for them at Barnes and Noble or your favorite bookstore

FERRY

FERRY takes you on an extraordinary journey over the Hudson River to the big city on a balmy fall day in the early 1950s. The trip across the narrows takes only few minutes but today you will live a lifetime during that trip as you join, Angelo Marullo, the shoeshine and all of the "regulars." They've got stories to tell and adventures to live out when they reach the big city. Want to know more? Well, there's a seat right over there by the window waiting for you!

LITTLE BOY BOO

Here's the story of a little Yorkshire terrier who thought he was a boy. *LIT-TLE BOY BOO* is a wonderful interactive book that is perfect for the child in your life. Whether you are a teacher, parent or grandparent, this unique little text offers the young reader the opportunity to become the book's Illustrator. There are games and puzzles to support reading comprehension and word meaning. At the end of the book there are lined pages for the child to create an original story. On the back cover the child gets affix a picture and write his/her own biography! There's never been a child's story book like this before! Great for the home…terrific for the classroom!

Dr. Mercaldo has visited many schools as a guest author and if you are a parent, teacher or school administrator an "Author Visit" is but a phone call away. Book him now for the coming year!

SEAMSTRESS

Is it possible for a friendship to really last a life-time? *SEAMSTRESS* literally "sews" together the lives of five women who were determined to let nothing get in the way of their friendship. They were destined to share their lives for as long as God gave them breath. Mercaldo has captured the essence of human bonding like no other writer today! *SEAMSTRESS* is testimony to this accomplishment. This is a story of mid-twentieth century life in America, when the "dream" was alive, and there for the taking; when the family was found in a house of worship on Sunday morning and a "million" family members sat around the dinner table! America sewed! We knitted, crocheted and twisted yarn in more creative ways than imaginable! But there was also the seamstress. They came in all kinds of shapes, colors and sizes! She was your grandmother, aunt, mother, cousin, sister, and friend. They were all there passing the pieces of every kind of garment under the arm of the sewing machine. Yes, David Mercaldo has captured an era when Americans looked to the future and dreamed!

FAMIGLIA

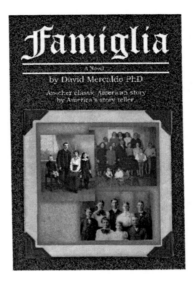

Dr. David Mercaldo's, *FAMIGLIA*, packs an emotional wallop. There are ironies and coincidences, triumphs and tragedies on this epic journey…a rich tapestry of hope in the new land. Meet Aldo, Vincente, Marcello and Giovanni, immigrant newcomers to New York City. Watch them defy their helplessness with determination and grit…like Jonah in the belly of the whale they manage to survive and thrive.

Their spiral upward involves abandoning boyhood dreams, embracing realities and persevering. They part with old traditions and learn to embrace their new life in America.

OFFICER'S OATH

OFFICER'S OATH is a story that everyone should read.

Here's the story of a man, Lt. Col. Dr. Terry Lakin who made a principled decision to adhere to the oath he willingly took as an officer in the United States Army. It is a story of the personal consequences of that decision and the far-reaching effect it has had on the eligibility issue. David Mercaldo, a New York-based author, has interviewed and written vignettes of the many people who contributed to Terry's case. A number of notable individuals have also contributed essays on key subjects relating to the issue. The book is a complete story of Terry's decision, the immediate consequences, and the long-range effect of Terry's life-changing decision and should generate a substantive and engaging dialogue on the issues addressed. Overall it is a unique book and an engaging story. Initial readers have given it high marks. It will be of great interest to supporters, detractors, and those who may have had little contact with the issues for which Terry has stood.

Visit DavidMercaldo.com

Visit David's website for the latest news about his books
and to submit requests for speaking engagements.

For Bookings Call 917 597 6055 or write -skyline347@verizon.net